My dearest Son Max,

On your sixth Birthday
so as to remember:
You are what you
resolve to be!

If your heart chooses
the lights of a siren,
I will support that or
any decision your future
holds.

Love & Happy
Birthday
your Dad

POLICE CARS
IN ACTION

Robert Genat

MBI Publishing Company

Dedication
To Mickey Kress, my good friend from the flatlands of Michigan.

First published in 1999 by MBI Publishing Company, 729 Prospect Avenue, PO Box 1, Osceola, WI 54020-0001 USA

MBI Publishing Company books are also available at discounts in bulk quantity for industrial or sales-promotional use. For details write to Special Sales Manager at Motorbooks International Wholesalers & Distributors, 729 Prospect Avenue, PO Box 1, Osceola, WI 54020-0001 USA.

Printed in Hong Kong

Library of Congress Cataloging-in-Publication Data

Genat, Robert
    Police cars in action / Robert Genat
    p. cm. (Enthusiast color series)
    Includes index.
    ISBN 0-7603-0521-8 (pbk. : alk. paper)
    1. Police vehicles--United States 2. Police pursuit driving--United States I. Title.
    II. Series
    HV7936.V4G48 1999
    629.2'088'3632--dc21   99-13090

On the front cover: The "black-and-white" has been an icon for law enforcement for decades. The traditional paint scheme on this Ford Crown Victoria makes it instantly recognizable to law-abiding citizens and law-breakers, alike.

On the frontispiece: Reserved parking.

On the title page: With many hours spent inside, the patrol car is the police officer's home away from home. While it needs to be comfortable, the patrol car must also provide the officer with performance and reliability.

On the back cover: This officer is using his patrol car's public address system to talk to an armed suspect in the doorway of a house. The car is positioned to offer the officer the greatest possible amount of protection from the suspect.
James J. Genat

Edited by Tracy Snyder and Christopher Batio

Designed by Dan Perry

Contents

Acknowledgments

There's only one way to do a book like this, and it's with the cooperation of police officers who serve our local communities. Most of my research took place in a police car (during many "ride-along" adventures) or sitting with officers as they shared their training experiences, war stories, and opinions on human behavior. Sitting next to a patrol officer working his or her beat is a great way to observe the real world of law enforcement. It's too bad everyone can't do a ride-along. If you could, I'm sure you would come away feeling the same level of pride I feel for our police officers.

Thanks to the following police, sheriffs', state police, and highway patrol departments that stepped up to help me with this book. A special thanks to all the law enforcement officers who freely gave of their time and took me into their confidence.

At the San Diego (California) Police Department, I would like to thank Chief Jerry Sanders, Assistant Chief John Welter, Lieutenant Bill Brown, and Officers Chuck Shipler and Joe Lopez.

At the California Highway Patrol (CHP), I want to thank Commissioner Spike Helmick; Commander Kent Milton; Assistant Chief Fred Norton; Captain Dave Kissinger; Lieutenant Mike Alduenda; and State Traffic Officers Dave Dreher, Micky Daley, Bill Grant, and Dave Ellison. A special thanks goes to State Traffic Officer Rick Sablan, Public Affairs Officer at the Oceanside, California, CHP station.

At the Escondido (California) Police Department, my thanks go out to Chief Duane White; Captain Lynn Nelson; Sergeant Geoff Galindo; Officers Doug Sams, Steve Jennings, Chris Lick, Scott Christensen, Stephen Thompson, and Ricardo Rodriguez; and dispatcher Gina Stark.

At the Carlsbad (California) Police Department, I would like to thank Lieutenant Dale Stockton and dispatcher Laura Irwin.

At the San Bernardino (California) Sheriffs' Department Emergency Vehicle Operations Center (EVOC), I want to thank Lieutenant Fred Daily and instructors Bob Rose, Scott Mahler, and Ed Curtis.

At the San Diego County Sheriffs' Department, I thank Sergeant Bert Quick, Deputy Ken Simon, and "Boris."

At the Michigan State Police, I wish to thank Lieutenant Camille Kleinow; Lieutenant Ed Hay; Sergeant Tom Pokora; Sergeant David Halliday; Sergeant Dennis Sano; and Troopers Stephen Anderson, John Duffy, and Keith Sparks.

At the Bloomfield Township (Michigan) Police Department, I'd like to thank Captain Reed Altenberg and Officer Donald Uppleger.

At the Holley (Michigan) Police Department, I would like to thank Officers Gregory Bowman and Buster Winebrenner.

At the Manassa (Colorado) Police Department I would like to thank Chief Dale Ruff.

At the Auburn Hills (Michigan) Police Department, I would like to thank Chief Doreen Olko; Lieutenant James Mynsberge; Sergeants Glenn Heath, James Manning, and Michael O'Hala; and Officers Kenneth Oman, Joan Badalucco, Jill McDonnel, Tracy Brdygs, and Liam Starrs, Patrick Becker and Jim Sparre.

At the Indiana State Police, I would like to thank Sergeant Joe Rhodes and Trooper Tim Wood.

Thanks to the many folks at Chevrolet and Ford who provided me with technical assistance on their cars, and thanks to Paul McMahon at LoJack.

A special thanks to James Genat and Dale Stockton for sharing their photos.

Introduction

We are at Deer Springs Road, the northern end of California Highway Patrol (CHP) Officer Dave Dreher's beat along I-15. He had just made the turn onto the entrance ramp to re-enter the southbound lanes when our conversation stops midsentence. We both see the red BMW streaking along in the number-one lane. Officer Dreher, already in second gear, eases the Mustang's throttle down, and we start to accelerate. I keep my mouth shut, tug on my seat belt, and squeeze the door armrest handle with my right hand. The engine's rpm rises to its peak and falls as Officer Dreher works the five-speed shifter. By the time we reach the end of the ramp, the red BMW is a dot on the horizon. We are close to 100 miles per hour and are still accelerating. At these speeds, the Mustang's throaty exhaust tone is left behind, replaced by the sound of the wind whistling around the windshield. Dreher's eyes are focused on the distant violator and traffic ahead as we continue to pick up speed.

For a fleeting second, I don't think we are going to catch this guy. We are now passing law-abiding motorists at 50 miles per hour faster than they are going. The Mustang's healthy 302 engine isn't even breaking a sweat at 110. Finally, we start to close on the violator, who is oblivious to the fact that a black-and-white police car is stalking him. Now within striking range, Officer Dreher positions his Mustang off of the BMW's right rear quarter panel, in the driver's blind spot. Officer Dreher, rock steady, paces the BMW at 95 miles per hour. Dreher then slips directly behind the BMW and lights him up.

I see the BMW driver look in his mirror. I silently pray that he will pull over. While I like speed, the thought of an extended high-speed chase is out of my realm of reality. The speeding driver looks into his mirror again and eases off the gas. I am finally able to exhale the deep breath I've been holding since we entered the freeway. Dreher is a pro—I'm sure his heart rate didn't get over 65 beats per minute.

The police-package Mustangs always rated well in high-speed tests. When tested, this 1993 model had a top speed of 137 miles per hour and would trip the quarter-mile clocks in 15.22 seconds. It was this kind of performance that prompted the California Highway Patrol to use the Mustang for freeway patrol.

Once stopped on the shoulder, Officer Dreher gets out of the Mustang and carefully approaches the BMW. Once he's confident that the driver is not a threat, he looks back my way. This is my signal to get out of the car and stand on the shoulder of the road. Cars (even police cars) sitting on the shoulder are often targets for drunk drivers. Statistics show that it's more likely that a police officer will be killed by road traffic than by a felon. The stop is uneventful, and the driver graciously accepts his speeding citation.

Riding in a police car during a pursuit is much different than watching it on TV. Every sense is heightened as your adrenaline pumps and heart rate increases. As you're approaching traffic, you pray that the car you're about to overtake is not going to suddenly change lanes. You also hope that all the mechanical parts on your car function properly. Any failure could spell disaster.

Part of my research for this book included riding along on patrol with several different departments. Some days were very busy, and others were, at times, boring. The one thing I came away with was a great deal of respect for the law enforcement officers I met. They approach their job with professionalism and pride. They have a tough job, and they do it well.

Your ride-along is about to get underway. Tighten your seat belt; we're going to take a look at *Police Cars in Action*.

1

POLICE CRUISERS

The patrol car is the officer's home and office, and it must be comfortable and safe. Not surprisingly, then, today's police cars are among the best-engineered law enforcement vehicles ever produced; they provide a high degree of occupant safety, vehicle performance, and reliability.

The look of police cars is continually changing. Several types of patrol cars have been phased out by the manufacturers over the past few years. Ford Motor Company no longer produces a police package for its fabled Mustang pony car or for its Taurus, discontinued in 1993 and 1995, respectively. In 1996, Chevrolet stopped production of one of the most successful police cars of all time: the LT1-powered Caprice.

With these popular packages no longer available, what will police cars of the future look like and have to offer? A newer option popular with some departments is the police-package Sport Utility Vehicle. This type of vehicle, though, does not have approval of the majority. While ideal for canine units, they lack the high-speed performance of the aerodynamically slick sedans. While styling may change over the years, full-sized sedans, it seems, are destined to be *the* choice by officers

In addition to many off-road vehicles, the U.S. Border Patrol also uses a fleet of patrol cars. This Chevy Caprice is used to pursue suspected illegal immigrants on the highway.

In 1992, Ford redesigned the Crown Vic. Its smooth new shape produced an impressive 0.34 drag coefficient. Also new for the 1992 model were four-wheel disc brakes, speed-sensitive power steering, passenger-side air-bag option, and optional ABS. The new roofline and many other parts carried through the 1997 model.

nationwide, particularly those with conventional rear-wheel drive. Front-wheel-drive cars, while well-engineered and very capable machines, never captured the hearts of the officers on the street.

Features

Whatever the manufacturer or style of the vehicle, police-option packages all have some of the same features available. A heavy-duty cooling system is one of the most important upgrades in a police car, given how extended periods of idling with both the air conditioner and lights on tax

the cooling system. Likewise, running at full throttle during an extended high-speed pursuit builds a lot of heat in the engine and transmission that could cause them to fail if the heat isn't bled off quickly. So heavy-duty radiators are standard, along with engine oil coolers and transmission coolers. More durable silicone radiator hoses and special clamps are also available.

During a pursuit, the siren, radio, and emergency lights are all activated, and the air conditioner may be running. This puts an extraordinary demand on the electrical system. Heavy-duty alternators with an output as high as 130 amps are available; compare this to passenger-car 100-amp-or-less units.

When police-package patrol cars are delivered to a department, they're already set up for the accessories that each department may want to add. Fused accessory wire feeds are available for radios, lights, and sirens, which allow each department to quickly outfit its cars as required. The factory can prewire the door pillars for spotlights, so departments can easily install the lights themselves, or the spotlights can be installed at the factory. Radio antenna cables routed through the roof are available as an option, as are roof supports for departments that will be fitting lightbars to the roof. A variety of power-window and power-door lock options are available, depending on the use of the car. A sergeant's or lieutenant's car may have the same system as a standard passenger car, but a patrol car that regularly transports suspects will most likely have all windows operated from the driver's seat only. Patrol cars also usually lack inside rear door handles, to help keep suspects inside.

The 1998 Crown Vic received a more formal grille and a revised roofline. It was also fitted with P225/60R16-97V performance tires on 8-inch-wide wheels. A small center cap (shown) or a full-wheel cover was available.

In 1995, Ford added a new chrome mesh grille to the Crown Vic that carried through the 1997 model. The Crown Vic has always been adaptable to the large variety of specialized equipment added to police cars.

Officers from two different agencies stop for a moment to discuss a recent accident to which they both responded. Both are driving Ford Crown Victorias painted in their respective departments' colors. *James J. Genat*

Because the air-bag deployment zones have taken away space formerly used to mount radios, shotguns, and radar equipment, all police cars are equipped with driver and passenger bucket seats equipped with antistab panels to prevent a rear-seat passenger from doing harm to the officers in the front. Front seats are typically cloth covered for comfort, and the floor is carpeted, while easy cleanup dictates a vinyl bench seat and rubber floor mat in the rear.

Typically, for the officer's safety, the interior lights of police cars don't automatically illuminate when the door is opened. At night, a fully illuminated interior makes an inviting target to someone wishing to harm an officer. The lack of automatic lighting also makes it easier for an officer's eyes to transition from a dark car to a low-light situation on the street.

The door, ignition, glovebox, and trunk locks on a police car are keyed to a single key. If desired, an entire department's fleet of cars can be keyed to a single key, which allows any of the department's officers to unlock a car, whether it's assigned to them or not. Any officer can place a prisoner in the most convenient car or retrieve a shotgun from the nearest patrol car.

Through 1995, Ford offered three different police cars: the Taurus, the Mustang, and the Crown Vic. Today they only offer the Crown Vic. Powered by a 4.6-liter, single-overhead-cam V-8 engine, the Crown Vic is capable of a 129-mile-per-hour top speed.

In 1998, Ford redesigned the rear suspension of the Crown Vic. A Watts linkage was added for enhanced lateral stability. An optional handling package offers heavier stabilizer bars and a 3.27:1 rear axle ratio. *James J. Genat*

Last, a rubber mat lines the trunk floor, where there is also a full-size spare tire in the larger sedans.

While the options available on all police packages are similar, the vehicles themselves differ in numerous ways. In recent years, the most popular packages have been produced by Ford and Chevrolet for their full-size sedans. Although some of these packages have been discontinued for future purchase, following are details on some of the more prevalent vehicles that patrol the streets today, along with a brief look at a variety of other vehicles that have been suited up for public service.

Crown Victoria

At present, Ford Motor Company has command of the full-size police-car market with its very successful Crown Victoria, better known as the Crown Vic. The current, aerodynamically slick version debuted in February 1992, replacing the boxier Crown Vic that was introduced in 1979.

When the 1992 Crown Vic was released, it differed radically from the previous model. The newer Crown Vic was well-rounded with an excellent 0.34 drag coefficient. Also released in 1992 for the Crown Vic were four-wheel disc brakes, speed-sensitive power steering, and a passenger-side air-bag option.

The antilock braking system (ABS) was a $600 option that most departments passed up, partially due to the cost of the option and partially due to the controversy over ABS in Chevrolet's Caprice (discussed later). Included with the Crown Vic's ABS was a traction-control system that senses the speed differential between the front and rear wheels. If the system detects slippage, it pulses the rear brakes. This traction-control system only operates at speeds under 35 miles per hour.

The 1992 Crown Vic was powered by Ford's then-new 4.6-liter, single-overhead-cam engine, rated at 210 horsepower, which replaced the 1991 model's 351-cubic-inch (5.8-liter) V-8 but produced 30 more horsepower

14

despite the decreased displacement. The 1992 4.6-liter V-8 was the first of Ford's "modular" engine designs, the long-range plans for which included increased displacement and multiple-valve configurations.

The 1992 Crown Vic's 4.6-liter V-8 engine was equipped with sequential multiport electronic fuel injection and Ford's EEC-V electronic engine controls. Backing this high-tech powerplant was an automatic transmission that featured electronically-controlled shift points and an overdrive fourth gear that could be manually locked out by the driver.

The performance levels of the new 4.6-liter V-8 engine were better than those of the 5.8-liter Crown Vics of the previous years, but not up to the level of the Chevy Caprice. The Crown Vic could reach 100 miles per hour in 28.6 seconds, but the 350-cubic-inch V-8-powered Caprice took only 25.9 seconds. Road-course lap times during the Michigan State Police tests also showed the Crown Vic to be slightly slower than the Caprice. Even though the 1992 Crown Vic didn't post the performance numbers of the Chevy Caprice, it still provided law enforcement with an extremely effective patrol vehicle and was purchased by many departments.

In 1994, Ford revised the car's disc brakes by adding angled vents to the rotors. Dual front air bags became standard too. In 1995, a revision to the EEC-V engine control computer improved the Crown Vic's performance. These changes allowed the Crown Vic to reach a top speed of 132 miles per hour. In the 1996 Michigan State Police tests, the 2-ton Crown Vic upped its terminal speed to 135, which was commendable, considering its 281-cubic-inch engine.

The Crown Vic remained relatively unchanged with only minor mechanical and cosmetic updates until the 1998 models were

Police cars often sit at idle for extended periods of time with lights, radios, and air conditioners all running. Ford engineers have developed heavy-duty cooling and electrical systems to handle the most demanding conditions.

released with a facelift that featured a more contemporary look. A Watts linkage rear suspension improved handling and straight-line stability while the new dual-piston front brake calipers enhanced braking. New 16-inch wheels mounting P225/60R16-97V all-season tires further enhanced handling and braking. An antilock braking system (ABS) was available as an option. The traction-control system—to which the ABS is linked—now operates at all speeds. Powering the 1998 Crown Vic is the same 4.6-liter V-8 engine first seen in 1992, but its horsepower has steadily increased to 215.

Chevrolet Caprice

Bar none, the 1996 Chevrolet Caprice was the best police car ever produced. That strong statement is backed by reams of departmental test data and police officers' opinions. The

1996 Caprice offered unequaled performance, along with all the room necessary for the largest officer. Unfortunately, 1996 was also the last year for the Caprice sedan. The story of the 1996 Caprice, however, actually begins in 1991, when the series was debuted.

The 1991 Caprice was an aerodynamically shaped replacement for the boxy Caprice that was introduced in 1977. The new Caprice featured a windshield with a slope of 62.5 degrees, which, along with a more rounded front fascia, dropped the drag coefficient to 0.327—the best ever for a full-size Chevy. Upon its release, the new Caprice was not a critical success, however. People found the new styling a dramatic departure from Chevrolet's formal look of the previous 13 years. The small wheel openings in the rear made the quarter panels look larger and wider than they actually were, and the whalelike appearance didn't set well with officers who liked their cars to perform well and to look good too. The small rear wheel openings also created a problem for mechanics when they wanted to remove the rear wheels with the car on a rack. It couldn't be done. The weight of the vehicle had to be off of the rear axle so the tire would drop low enough in the wheel opening to be removed.

The chassis under the 1991 Caprice remained the same as the 1990 model, with the addition of front discs and rear drum brakes. Also new were antilock brakes, available for the first time in a police car; however, unfamiliarity with the advantages of ABS technology caused some problems for Chevrolet. Some departments made claims that the system was faulty

When Chevrolet released the 1991 Caprice, it was the object of much discussion because of its shape, which was a drastic departure from the previous Caprice's styling. Department mechanics didn't like the new rear-wheel openings because they couldn't easily remove the rear tires.

Michigan State Police Vehicle Evaluations

Performance data on police cars is important to agencies when they purchase new patrol cars, and one of the best sources of this type of information is the Michigan State Police vehicle test reports.

Every year since 1976, the Michigan State Police has evaluated law enforcement vehicles. The Michigan State Police began these tests to determine which of the police vehicles being offered had the performance capabilities (high speed, handling, and braking) they required. The tests have continued, and today, the Michigan State Police vehicle test is the largest law enforcement evaluation in North America.

In 1998, 500 law enforcement officers, officials, and fleet administrators from large and small departments gathered to observe the 13 1999 vehicles being tested by Michigan State Police officers. The observers were allowed to watch the cars on the track and to see the results as they were tabulated. They also had a chance to talk to the manufacturers' engineering representatives who attend to support their companies' vehicles.

Actual testing takes place over three days in three different locations. Two days of high-speed, braking, and handling evaluations take place at the Chrysler proving grounds in Chelsea, Michigan, and at the Michigan International Speedway in Brooklyn, Michigan. A third day, spent at the Michigan State Police Academy in Lansing, is devoted to ergonomics and communications testing. All vehicles are subjected to the same rigorous tests. The goal of the evaluations is to determine the best-performing patrol car from a performance standpoint. The lowest bidder (the traditional government purchasing benchmark) may not always have the best-performing patrol car. Once the testing is completed, the results are available at no cost from the National Institute of Justice to any law enforcement agency that requests them.

Vehicles included in the Michigan State Police evaluations are those that are marketed and sold as a police vehicle by their manufacturers. The 13 included in the 1999 evaluations were split into two categories. Ten were classified as "police vehicles," and three were listed as "special service." Police vehicles are those that the manufacturer affirms are capable of high-speed and pursuit driving, while special service vehicles are those with attributes that make them worthy of consideration by law enforcement but are not suitable for pursuit or high-speed driving such as pickup trucks and most SUVs.

The Los Angeles County Sheriffs' Department also conducts an annual evaluation of law enforcement vehicles. Its tests include high-speed and braking performance evaluations similar to those conducted by the Michigan State Police. But they also test the upper limits of the vehicle's cooling systems—a requirement for any police vehicle operating in the southwestern portion of the nation.

In 1993, the Caprice's rear-wheel openings were revised, giving the car a much more aggressive look. In 1994 the LT1 engine was added, making the Caprice the fastest full-size police car ever produced, capable of speeds in excess of 140 miles per hour. This 1996 model is assigned to the California Highway Patrol.

and that the cars didn't stop as well as those without ABS. But Chevrolet knew its system worked and discovered that the officers driving these cars needed to be trained in the proper use of ABS. To clear up the issue, Chevrolet produced a video that clearly showed the advantages of the system over standard brakes and also emphasized that the officers needed to change their way of braking in a car with ABS—they needed to stop pumping the brakes.

The 1991 Caprice was also the first Chevy police car equipped with a driver's-side air bag. As with ABS, many officers were skeptical of this pyrotechnic device located inches away from their face. Chevrolet responded to their concerns by producing a videotape on the new Supplemental Restraint System. Statistics substantiated the fact that lives were saved with the air-bag system.

Another improvement on the 1991 Caprice came via the new aerodynamic shaping. Even though the 1991 Caprice had the same engine as the previous year, it performed better. The slippery shape cut through the wind, allowing the new Caprice to reach a top speed of 130 miles per hour—8 miles per hour faster than the boxier 1990 model. Powering the 1991 Caprice was a throttle-body-injected, 350-cubic-inch "small-block" Chevrolet V-8 that produced 195 horsepower. Also available in the 1991 Caprice was the 170-horsepower 305-cubic-inch engine.

For 1992, Chevrolet upped the horsepower of the 350-cubic-inch engine to 205, with the installation of a low-restriction exhaust system and new fresh-air intake. The performance increase was noted in both the Michigan State Police and Los Angeles County

Sheriffs' tests, where the Caprice's quarter-mile times improved by over two-tenths of a second. The 1992 Caprice was also the leader in the top-speed category, clocking 133 miles per hour—9 miles per hour faster than Ford's 1992 Crown Vic.

In 1993, Chevrolet redesigned the rear quarter panels to provide full-wheel openings. This single change dramatically improved the appearance of the car and made the mechanics happy who had to remove the rear tires. The braking system also benefited from major improvements, including a refined ABS system that provided better performance on rough surfaces plus longer-lasting friction materials for both the front and rear brakes.

The powerful LT1 Corvette engine became part of the Caprice police package in 1994. With 260 horsepower, it provided the punch to make the Caprice the fastest police sedan ever! It even posted better acceleration times than the fabled 5.0 police Mustang. The new Caprice clocked a top speed of 141 miles per hour in the Michigan State Police tests—12 miles per hour faster than the Ford Taurus. Only Chevy's B4C Camaro eclipsed the Caprice's speed with its astounding 153-mile-per-hour top end.

Redesigned cylinder heads, ignition improvements, and the addition of sequential port fuel injection were responsible for the increase in horsepower. Backing the LT1 engine was GM's 4L60-E electronic-overdrive transmission, which was reprogrammed for police use with firmer upshift and lower downshift points. At wide-open throttle, the police-package LT1

Many police departments were disappointed to hear that Chevrolet was halting production of the Caprice at the end of the 1996 model year. Numerous letters were sent to General Motors requesting the continuation of the model. To meet the demands of the departments, GM extended the production of the police-version Caprice during that last year.

When first released, the Taurus was the first of a new generation of aerodynamically-designed American cars. Its sleek shape and 160-horsepower engine allowed the Taurus to reach a top speed of 129 miles per hour.

Caprice's transmission shifted from third to fourth at 120 miles per hour—a speed not even attainable by most passengers cars of the era.

There were several more improvements to the 1994 Caprice, including four-wheel disc brakes, which augmented the ABS. Chevrolet always had a problem retaining full-size wheel covers on the Caprice, especially during hard cornering on high-speed pursuits. In 1994, Chevrolet gave up on standard full-size wheel covers and added a small bolt-on hub cover to the center of the wheel. Along with the wide wheels and P225/70-15 tires, this small hub cover added an aggressive look to the cars. The 1994 Caprice was also equipped with dual air bags, which forced departments to reposition shotgun mounts, Mobile Data Terminals

(MDTs), radar units, and radios out of the passenger-side air bag's deployment zone. For the 1994 civilian market, Chevrolet took the police-package Caprice and added leather seats, 17-inch alloy wheels, and SS logos to the quarter panels to create the Impala SS. It was a rousing success—Chevrolet quickly sold every one it manufactured.

The 1995 Caprice was a carryover of the 1994 model with one minor change to the exterior: the door-mounted side-view mirrors were relocated to the front lower corner of the window frame and were a breakaway design.

The 1996 Caprice police package was the last and best of the breed. A few technical improvements were added to upgrade the performance and durability. Unfortunately, just when Chevrolet finally got it all right, they pulled the plug on the program. On May 17, 1995, *USA Today* reported the bad news in an article titled "GM Scraps Big Cars." The Arlington, Texas, plant that produced the Caprice would be converted to manufacturing highly profitable trucks. The production run of the Caprice would officially end on December 13, 1996. Because of the popularity of the car, many departments wrote to Chevrolet requesting that it not stop production. In an effort to appease the waiting market, Chevrolet produced an additional 25,000 police-package Caprices in 1996.

An interesting sidebar to the demise of the 1996 Caprice was the effort of RCI, Inc., a Michigan-based company that outfits police cars, which wanted to buy the tooling for the Caprice to continue production of the popular sedan at a factory in Canada. General Motors refused, and the Caprice was laid to rest.

But the Caprice story may not be over. It is rumored that Chevrolet is going to produce another full-size sedan for the year 2000. It's supposed to have all the interior room of the 1996 Caprice with a slightly smaller exterior.

Ford Taurus and Chevrolet Lumina

The Ford Taurus and Chevrolet Lumina are the two most popular front-wheel-drive sedans being used for law enforcement work today. Both are well-engineered and capable vehicles. The Ford Taurus was first available with a police package in 1990, and Chevy's Lumina joined it in 1992.

When the first Taurus police-package vehicle was tested in 1990, it amazed a lot of people. It was fast and handled much better

Ford's Taurus police package offered solid handling, good acceleration, and an excellent top speed. Unfortunately, it was a front-wheel-drive design, and most police officers still prefer rear-wheel-drive cars. The police-package Taurus was last produced in 1995.

Today, Chevrolet's Lumina is the only front-wheel-drive police car offered. It features a 3.8-liter V-6, rated at 200 horsepower. Recaro front bucket seats are standard.

than imagined. Powered by a 3.8-liter V-6, the Taurus was faster than the then-current 5.8-liter Crown Vic and had a better braking system, as well. Many departments that had previously overlooked the Taurus began placing orders.

In 1991, Ford brought its Taurus to the Michigan State Police tests with an engine bristling with 15 additional horsepower. The 1991 Taurus posted the quickest lap times on the road course. On the high-speed portion of the test, it hit 129.4 miles per hour—only the new 5.7-liter Caprice bested that speed (and just barely) at 130 miles per hour. On the 0 to 100 dash, the V-6 Taurus was a full 5 seconds faster than the 5.8-liter Crown Vic.

Nineteen ninety-five was the last year for the Taurus police package. Even though the Taurus performed well, it was never popular with the officers in the field who prefer rear-wheel-drive vehicles.

The first Chevy Lumina police package was released for the 1992 model year, but it wasn't Chevrolet's first front-wheel-drive police car: between 1984 and 1986, Chevrolet had offered its Celebrity with a police package. The 1992 Lumina police package was a direct response to Ford's 1991 Taurus that had tested so well at the Michigan State Police tests. Powering Chevy's Lumina was a 140-horsepower 3.1-liter V-6 engine, which drove through a four-speed transaxle with a final-drive ratio of 3.33:1. Top speed for the Lumina at the Michigan State Police tests was 111 miles per hour. To reach 100 miles per hour from a standing start, it took the Lumina 41.9 seconds—the slowest of the cars tested that year. While short on speed, the Michigan State Police testers were pleased with the car's handling and braking ability.

The 1993 police-package Lumina featured aluminum wheels and Recaro bucket seats, with the same drivetrain as the previous year. The Lumina police package wasn't available in 1994, but it returned in 1995 with a redesigned body, a new rear suspension, and improved performance.

The 1995 Lumina featured a much sleeker body than the previous model, but the major improvements occurred under the hood. Powering the 1995 Lumina was a 3.1-liter V-6 with a new roller camshaft, revised intake plenum, better-flowing heads, and higher 9.6:1 compression that all contributed to a 160 horsepower peak and increased performance. The 1995 Lumina could reach 100 miles per hour in 34.04 seconds—over 7 seconds faster than the 1992 model. Top speed was up 7 miles per hour to 118. The 1995 police Lumina also had rear disc brakes, which weren't available on the civilian Lumina.

For 1996, the Lumina received only minor engine changes, but top speed improved to

The Ford Expedition offers an excellent police package for off-road police work. Available in either 4x2 or 4x4 configuration, the Expedition can also fulfill many roles on city streets. *Dale Stockton*

122 miles per hour. Except for some minor changes, the 1997 Lumina was a carryover of the 1996 model. The 1998 model, however, featured more horsepower thanks to its 200-horsepower 3.8-liter V-6.

While both the Taurus and Lumina are very reputable police vehicles, it's a fact of life that police officers have always preferred rear-wheel-drive, full-size sedans. These cars have traditionally offered the maximum amount of interior room and the most powerful engines. Police officers also like the way rear-wheel-drive

cars perform when pushed to the limit. There's also the repair factor: When a police car gets into an accident, usually the front end is damaged, which can cause major—and expensive—damage to the transmission, drive shaft, and front struts. In addition, front-wheel-drive cars are constructed with a unitized body that is much more difficult to repair when heavily damaged.

But despite these factors, this doesn't diminish the capabilities of front-wheel-drive cars in law enforcement roles; both the Chevy

Even pickup trucks have found their way into police work. This GMC model is fitted with grille-mounted emergency lights and spotlights in the A-pillars. The two other police vehicles in the background are SUVs outfitted for canine use.

Lumina and the Ford Taurus perform admirably in service with departments across the country.

Sport Utes and Others

Sport Utility Vehicles, more commonly referred to as "Sport Utes" or "SUVs," have taken the country by storm. The high level of trim and options offered in SUVs has made them favorites of business people in place of luxury sedans. Because of the lack of full-size station wagons, police departments also have adapted the SUVs to suit their needs. Those currently offered with special service or police packages are the Jeep Cherokee, Chevy Tahoe, Ford Explorer, Ford Expedition, and Subaru Outback wagon. The fastest of the group is the Chevy Tahoe with a top speed of 123 miles per hour; the others max out at around 110.

Another trend of the future in police vehicles is cars from Volvo. In 1997, the folks at Volvo nudged their way into the domestic police-car market with their 850 sedan. Powered by a 2.3-liter, turbocharged, 222-horsepower engine, its performance surprised a lot of people. In the 1997 Michigan State Police tests, the Volvo reached a top speed of 145 miles per hour—the quickest of any four-door sedan tested. Its quarter-mile times were also the fastest of the sedans at 16.18 seconds and 88.9 miles per hour. In 1998, Volvo returned to the tests with its S-70 sedan. Its 2.3-liter engine now boasted 236 horsepower and pushed the sedan to a terminal velocity of 147 miles per hour. In the braking phase of the test, the Volvo ground to a halt from 60 miles per hour in 132.2 feet—a shorter distance than any other vehicle tested. It was clearly the class of the field. Because of its performance numbers, the new Volvo is being tested by several departments, including the California Highway Patrol.

Other nonpolice-package cars can occasionally be seen in service as well. Quite often a major auto manufacturer will offer cars to an individual department to test durability. In the past, it was not unusual to see a Lincoln Town Car or Ford Thunderbird in police livery for the Dearborn, Michigan, Police Department.

End of the Line

How long these various vehicles serve the public varies, depending on where they are in service. Each police department has a vehicle mileage limit at which it concludes the patrol car has used up its service life, usually between 100,000 and 120,000 miles. At this point, the cars are "turned-out"—a euphemism for being sold. The municipality where the cars were in service may put them up for bid to private citizens, they may be sold directly to another department, or they may be bought by one of several companies that specializes in refurbishing old police cars for smaller communities and even some foreign countries that may need to buy several cars and don't want the expense of new vehicles. Prior to being sold, all of the police special equipment—radar, lights, radios, and shotgun mounts—is removed. Quite often, this equipment is installed on the new patrol car coming into service.

Occasionally, an auto manufacturer will place selected models with various police departments to test the durability of the vehicle or certain options. These Dodge Intrepids regularly patrol the streets of Auburn Hills, Michigan. *James J. Genat*

2

HIGH-PERFORMANCE PATROL CARS

In the late 1970s, the phrase "performance car" was quickly fading from our lexicon. The Environmental Protection Agency's (EPA) emission restrictions and gas mileage concerns severely atrophied the performance of factory musclecars and factory police packages. The cars available for police work were lethargic at best. On the roads, the nationwide 55-mile-per-hour speed limit was regularly being exceeded. Catching a speeder was difficult because the police cars available could not accelerate much faster than a taxicab. Police and highway patrol units were soon to discover that a small, but powerful, solution was on the way in the form of high-performance patrol cars.

Ford Mustang

In 1981, the engineers at Ford Motor Company were faced with a challenge: They found out that General Motors was going to provide a 1982 Firebird and Camaro to the Michigan State Police for their annual vehicle evaluation. Knowing that, in 1979, the California Highway Patrol had purchased 12 Camaro Z28s, and knowing that the CHP was

In Southern California, cops and rodders have always had an affinity for each other. Here the owner of a chopped and channeled Model A Ford coupe is checking out a CHP Mustang, while the officer is doing the same with the hot rod.

Some officers found that the Mustang's interior lacked the comfort of a full-size police cruiser. But what it lacked in space, the Mustang made up for in performance. This particular Mustang is equipped with a manual transmission.

Opposite
Most Mustangs in police service were traffic-enforcement units used by highway patrol and state police departments. To catch a speeder, a police car needs quick acceleration and high-speed stability, both features of the Mustang. Most departments, like the CHP, ran their Mustangs "slick top," without a lightbar.

interested in the new GM pony car's performance, Ford prepared a Mustang for the tests to prevent GM from having the upper hand in the market segment. The first day of the evaluation, the Ford Mustang was the only pony car at the test—the GM cars were nowhere to be seen. The little Mustang proceeded to amaze the testers and observers with its performance. In 1982, the CHP ordered 406 police-package Mustangs at a cost of $6,868 each, forever changing the face of police patrol cars.

The 1982 Mustang police package (cataloged by Ford in 1982 as the "Severe Service Package") was a standard LX sedan. It had a 302-cubic-inch engine (rated at 157 horsepower) backed with a four-speed manual transmission. To get the power out of the engine, Ford installed a longer duration cam and a large two-barrel carburetor. This same engine was also offered to the general public in the Mustang. Added to the police package was GT suspension without the alloy wheels. Michigan State Police tests showed that the Mustang had excellent acceleration and top speed: from 0 to 60, it tripped the clocks at 8.35 seconds, and it ran the quarter mile in 15.96 seconds. The 1982 Mustang far outclassed the field with a top speed of 124.4 miles per hour.

The CHP's fleet of Mustangs was a success. In America's hot-rodding epicenter, the cops now had a hot rod too. Dave Ellison is a California Highway Patrol officer who graduated from the CHP Academy in 1981. When the Mustangs were introduced to the CHP in 1982, all the officers wanted to drive them, including Ellison. "It was a coveted car," says Ellison. "A lot of people wanted to drive the Mustang. After awhile, the newness wore off, and a lot of people didn't want to drive it, because they didn't like driving with the stick shift. It was a little bit more work, like any manual transmission." Ellison, though, always

Dave Ellison joined the California Highway Patrol in 1981. Like most other CHP officers, he wanted to drive the Mustang when it was introduced into the CHP's fleet in 1982. Because of its skittish suspension, some officers declined to drive the Mustang during inclement weather. Ellison, however, loved the way the Mustang performed and drove it rain or shine. Many officers, like Ellison, regretted Ford's decision to discontinue the police option when the new Mustang was introduced in 1994.

enjoyed driving the Mustang and found that citizens were always interested in it and asked questions about the car. "They'd ask how fast it was, what modifications were done to it, how often do you chase people, or do you ever lose anybody?" Ellison claims the Mustang was a very consistent-running car and very dependable.

In 1983, the Mustang's horsepower was increased to 175 with the addition of a four-barrel carburetor. Top speed jumped to 132 miles per hour, once again the best of any car tested by the Michigan State Police. In fact, it was the first police car to eclipse 130 miles per hour since the 1978 440-cubic-inch Mopar police sedans. Other agencies placed orders for Mustangs in 1983 because of the success of the CHP's Mustangs.

In 1984, the Mustang fleet again expanded with several more agencies adding them to their livery. The Mustang's acceleration and durability made it the favorite of troopers across the country. In 1984, Ford added an optional automatic transmission to the police Mustang. Also available for 1984 and 1985 was a fuel-injected version with a lower horsepower rating. In 1986, a new multiport fuel-injection system was added, and horsepower jumped to 200. Zero-to-60 times were down to 5.3 seconds, and the top speed was up to 137 miles per hour. Other than cosmetics and a few minor mechanical changes, the Mustang police package remained the same through 1993.

Over all the years of its production, the police-package Mustang had a very important feature—fast acceleration, the most important

Ford Motor Company offered a total-performance package with the Mustang. In addition to the strong-running 302 engine, the Mustang included a heavy-duty suspension and performance tires.

One of the keys to giving an officer the confidence to drive at speeds in excess of 100 miles per hour is excellent vehicle maintenance. Here a California Highway Patrol mechanic is giving a Mustang a tune-up.

feature of any patrol car. The key is how fast you can get to 65 or 70 miles per hour. "If you're on the shoulder and somebody passes you at 80, you've got to go from 0 to 80 and not lose sight of them," claims Ellison. "You want a fast car off the line—everything at the top is gravy." As a general rule, a police car must be able to average 20 miles per hour faster than the car being pursued to be able to overtake them in a reasonable amount of time. The Mustang had an abundance of acceleration.

But the Mustang wasn't perfect. It had flaws that prevented its widespread use. The interior room of the Mustang was limited, especially for any officer over 6 feet tall. It also lacked the rear-seat room for city work, where prisoners are regularly transported. Cages were never installed in the Mustang because its two-door configuration made installation impossible. One officer said he would transport intoxicated individuals in the back seat of his Mustang by belting them in the rear seat and moving the front seat as far back as it could go so the drunk's feet would be trapped. He'd then raise the headrest up to provide a barrier between him and his passenger. The officer also informed the passenger that if he were to get sick, he'd be responsible for cleaning the car. More often than not, a four-door unit was called to transport prisoners. In addition, trunk space in the Mustang was barely sufficient for the variety of equipment police officers need to carry.

Another drawback of the Mustang was its braking ability. The brakes on the Mustang were adequate for most police work, but on extended pursuits they would fade. "Every time I can remember being in a pursuit where I had to do repetitive hard braking in a Mustang, I experienced big-time brake fade—real bad," says CHP Officer Dave Dreher. "If I needed to slow down to a stop from 100 and I've already used the brakes hard within 30 seconds or a minute—stand by, you'd better be downshifting pretty fast to get slowed down."

An additional negative mark on the Mustang name was the numerous crashes in which they were involved. But to be honest, most of the officers who crashed drove beyond their and the car's capabilities. Driving in the rain has always been a problem with the Mustang because the rear is so light, and the cars easily spin out.

Not all officers experienced high-speed accidents, however. As CHP Officer Ellison points out, preparation and familiarity with the car can prevent such incidents. "You have to remember that the car's only as good as the driver," says Ellison. "I've been driving for the CHP since '81 and have not had one accident yet. As far as I'm concerned, the Mustang's my car, and I'm not going to change to another car because of weather conditions. I know how it handles on both wet and dry roads. It would be silly for me to get into another car I'm not used to and then go drive it in the rain. I know the negative aspects of the Mustang and can adjust for them."

Officer Ellison feels that one of the keys to being a good Mustang driver is driving a performance car while off-duty. "You can't get someone who drives a Cadillac off-duty to step into a Mustang and be comfortable with how it handles," scoffs Ellison. "It's like anything in life; if there's something you're comfortable with, it's hard to change. When I first started driving the Mustang, I drove a Nissan 280ZX with a five speed. I drove it hard, and when I came to work, I drove the Mustang hard."

Officer Ellison, driving a CHP Mustang, helped apprehend a robbery suspect who was fleeing on a motorcycle. "This guy had been

The small trunk on a police Mustang is typically filled to the brim with equipment. Included in this Mustang's trunk are road flares, rubber cones, a fire extinguisher, marking paint, a lug wrench, emergency blankets, a motor vehicle code book, and a first aid kit—all necessary items for any highway patrol unit.

The Chevrolet police-package Camaro has picked up where the Mustang left off. It's the fastest police car ever tested, capable of top speeds in excess of 150 miles per hour. In addition to being quick, the Camaro has knockout styling.

running a string of robberies in the area using the motorcycle as a getaway," says Ellison. "This particular night I got involved in the pursuit of this motorcycle. It was going so fast it was outrunning the helicopter. I didn't know what speed I was going, because I wasn't about to take my eyes off the road to look at the speedometer. When you're driving a car fast, your focus has got to be on the road ahead. I know it was as fast as I'd ever want to go in this car." The only police car that could stay with the suspect was the Mustang. The guy on the motorcycle eventually crashed.

Although many officers, such as Dave Ellison, found the Mustang to be an exemplary police vehicle, the car's days were numbered. In 1993, Ford produced the last Mustang police package. In 1994, when the redesigned Mustang appeared, Ford opted not to offer a police package, thereby ending a glorious and proud police career. Many officers nationwide were sorry to see their department's last Mustang turned out.

Chevrolet Camaro

As mentioned earlier, Ford wasn't the only car manufacturer that attempted to enter the police market with a pony car. In 1979, with the performance of the full-size police offerings in a downward spiral without any foreseeable chance of pulling out, Chevrolet actually made the initial move. They worked out a deal with the California Highway Patrol to sell them 12 new Z28 Camaros for evaluation. The news of the CHP's musclecar acquisition was featured in many automotive enthusiast magazines, which made the CHP's little coupe great for traffic enforcement and a valuable public relations asset.

The Camaros were lightweight and powerful, with a 160-horsepower 350-cubic-inch engine backed by the Turbo Hydra-matic transmission. The Camaros were delivered without the colorful Z28 graphics package offered on civilian cars and were painted black with black-painted styled steel wheels and white doors emblazoned with the CHP seven-point shield and the words "HIGHWAY PATROL" in a semicircle above. The Z28s were fitted with a pair of A-pillar spotlights and a pair of emergency lights mounted on the package tray, but no lightbar.

The new Z28s featured three modifications for their new role: the rear axle ratio was changed from 3.42:1 to 3.08:1 to give the car a higher top end and required an exemption from the California Air Resources Board; the brakes were upgraded with Nova police-package hardware, including front discs with metallic linings and finned rear

brake drums; and the Z28's standard steel-belted radial tires were replaced with police-specification Firestone fabric-belted tires because there was some concern about the durability of steel-belted radials during sustained high-speed pursuits.

Through the 1980s, a few other departments experimented with Camaros in police roles. Like those evaluated by the CHP, these vehicles were showroom models with modifications made to suit police-pursuit duty. Meanwhile, the Mustang pulled ahead in the police pony-car market with its Mustang, introduced in 1982. It wasn't until 1991 that

The police Camaro sports P245/50ZR16 tires mounted on 8-inch-wide alloy wheels. The brakes are four-wheel discs with standard ABS. Under the hood is a 350-cubic-inch V-8 that delivers 305 horsepower.

The police Camaro's main role is traffic enforcement, where its rabbit-quick acceleration reels in speeders in minimal time. Camaro's secondary role is public relations, where it's a big hit, especially with young people.

Chevrolet designed a true police package for the Camaro. The B4C Special Service Package was designed specifically as an option on the Camaro RS model. Two small-block V-8 engines were available: the 230-horsepower 305-cubic-inch V-8 with a five-speed manual or the 350-cubic-inch 245-horsepower V-8 mated to an automatic with overdrive. Both of these engines had Tuned Port Injection and a dual-outlet exhaust system.

At the Michigan State Police tests, the new Camaro recorded performance numbers in excess of the police-package Mustang. The 350-cubic-inch Camaro was a full 1.5 seconds quicker in the quarter mile, and its overall top speed was 150 miles per hour, compared to the Mustang's 136. Equipped with four-wheel disc brakes, the Camaro also out-braked the Mustang. But the Camaro lacked driver comfort, with a seat much lower than the Mustang's, which was tiresome for traffic officers who had to get in and out of their patrol cars five times an hour. The suspension was also stiffer than the Mustang's, contributing to driver fatigue over a long shift.

In 1992, Chevrolet upgraded the Camaro's already excellent brakes, adding Corvette discs and calipers. Performance numbers for the 1992 Camaro were essentially the same as those for the 1991 model.

In 1993, Chevrolet redesigned the Camaro. Under the stylish new outer sheet metal

Out of sight in the Camaro's cargo compartment are the electronic black boxes for the radio, siren, strobe lights, and data terminal. Just below, a Ruger carbine is securely locked in its rack. This equipment is hidden from inquisitive eyes by a heavily-tinted rear hatch window.

was an improved drivetrain and chassis. The engine was the Corvette's LT1 350-cubic-inch V-8, rated at 275 horsepower and available with either a six-speed manual transmission or a four-speed automatic transmission. The redesigned front suspension featured more wheel travel plus rack-and-pinion steering. Four-wheel disc brakes and ABS were standard. The new 1993 Camaro eclipsed the records at the Michigan State Police tests set by the previous Camaro. It reached a top speed of 154 miles per hour and had a quarter-mile

time of 14.69 seconds at a speed of 95.8 miles per hour. It was faster than any previous car tested through the slalom course and stopped on a dime. The new Camaro set unmatchable new standards for police cruisers. But would it fill the void left by the departing Mustang?

In 1994, with the demise of the police-package Mustang, the Camaro had the pony-car police market all to itself. Instead of resting on its laurels, Chevrolet continued to fine-tune the package. The fuel-injection system was converted from the multiport system to

This Camaro's lightbar is as sleek and stylish as the car itself. Rotating halogen lights are contained within the seven smooth plastic domes that are arranged in a V formation. This lightbar produces less aerodynamic drag than the standard lightbar.

sequential port injection, which broadened the power band and made the engine more responsive, though it remained rated at 275 horsepower. Other subtle tweaks were made to both the automatic and manual transmissions.

Once again the Camaro was the performance king at the Michigan State Police evaluations.

Although the 1995 police Camaro was a virtual carryover of the 1994 model, it increased its top speed to 155 miles per hour.

Most of the components that make up the Camaro police package are from the Z28. The electrical system is modified for the unique needs of law enforcement, and a certified speedometer is added. *James J. Genat*

In 1996, the law enforcement automotive focus was on the concluding chapter of the Caprice. Powered by an LT1 engine similar to the Camaro's, the Caprice had become a favorite of law enforcement officers. Sales of the Camaro actually suffered because of the Caprice's excellent performance. In 1996, the Camaro gained 10 horsepower, moving up to 285, through a revised camshaft and redesigned exhaust system. These changes boosted the Camaro's top speed to a blazing 159 miles per hour. The Acceleration Slip Regulation (ASR) traction-control option was also introduced this year.

The 1997 Camaro was a carryover of the 1996 model, but the 1998 model once again saw an increase in horsepower—to 305. The additional power dropped the quarter-mile elapsed times to 14.45 seconds, with a speed of 101.6 miles per hour. In 1998, the Michigan State Police felt it wasn't in the best interest of safety to record speeds in excess of 150 miles per hour. It was noted in their report, however, that the Camaro could have gone faster.

The police-optioned Camaro has always fought an uphill battle. When first released in 1991, Camaro butted heads with the well-established and accepted police Mustang. The current version suffers from sporty styling and excessive performance, and many cities shy away from buying the Camaro because bureaucrats are wary of citizens' questions about spending their city's money on a "flashy sports car" instead of on a traditional police sedan, though the facts show the Camaro—optioned with the same equipment as a traditional police sedan—actually costs less. And when it comes to catching speeders, the Camaro has no equal. Acceleration is the key to reduced pursuit times for any officer working traffic,

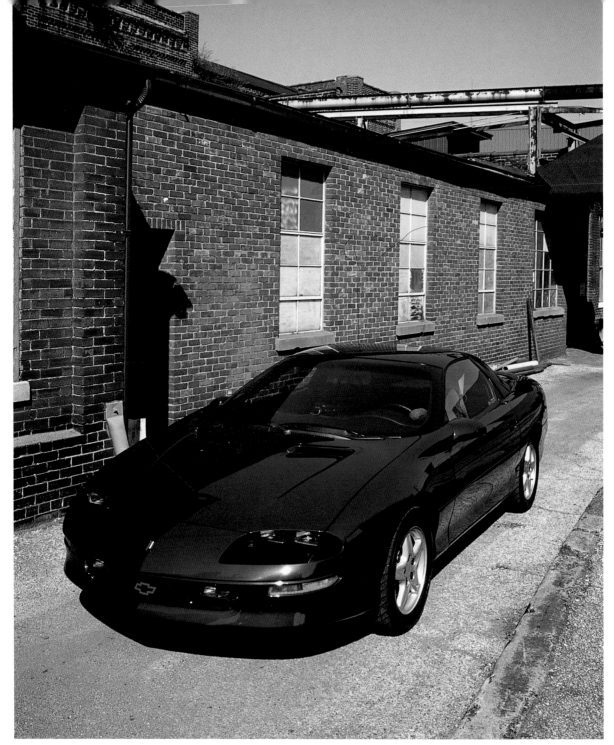

The small object on the driver's side of the instrument panel is one of the radar antennas. It's covered with a small piece of cloth to disguise it from unsuspecting motorists. The box on the center of the instrument panel is the readout for the radar.

Believe it or not, this Camaro *is* a police car. In 1988, the state of Indiana developed a special highway enforcement program with unmarked Mustangs. Today, the officers in this program drive Camaros in a variety of colors. These officers get to take the Camaros home and can drive them off-duty. Traffic stops and arrests (unless for a felony) can be made only when the officer is in uniform. Because of the type of car they drive, most officers in the program have at least one story to tell of someone challenging them to a race while off-duty.

and the Camaro is *fast*. "With the Camaro," says Traffic Officer Doug Sams of the Escondido, California, Police Department, "the chase is over before it ever begins."

There is one plus, however, that doesn't show on a bureaucrat's spreadsheet—the positive response the officers receive when they drive the Camaro. It's not unusual, while at a traffic light, for someone to smile and give the officer a thumbs-up. The Camaro is also an excellent public relations tool at events where young people attend, such as car shows and street fairs. Here, young men take time to speak

to the officer who drives the Camaro, and in many cases, it may be their first chance to talk to a police officer in a nonconfrontational manner.

The police-package Mustangs and Camaros filled a void created by poorly performing police sedans. Since the introduction of these police pony cars, the performance of the larger sedans has steadily improved, thereby reducing the need for a pint-sized patrol car. Rumors abound regarding GM's cancellation of the F-body Camaro and Firebird. If that's true, it will mean an end to some of the coolest and fastest police cars ever produced.

41

SPECIAL EQUIPMENT

What do most people think of when they hear the term "police car?" Images of flashing lights and blaring sirens immediately come to mind. And what about the fuzzy crackle of a radio as officers communicate with one another in law enforcement lingo? Lights, sirens, radios, and much more are important accessories that turn an otherwise normal vehicle into an effective police tool. Manufacturers put a great deal of engineering into their police vehicles to allow individual departments to easily add the types of accessories that best suit their needs. Other accessories include radar, push bars, cages, video cameras, guns, MDTs, and external identification markings—all important elements that help equip today's police cars.

Markings

One of the most visible modifications to the police car is its markings. A few years ago, the trend toward brightly colored graphics on police cars was on the rise. Today, police cars with brilliantly colored reflective graphics mix with the customary black-and-white paint scheme that was first seen in the 1930s. The colorful reflective-tape markings have made the patrol cars highly visible, but reviews from officers in the field were often mixed. Many felt that the average citizen could readily notice

Who says that a black-and-white patrol car is boring? The sleek lines of the Camaro lend themselves well to this inspired graphic design. *James J. Genat*

43

With the exception of a few special-purpose cars, all California Highway Patrol vehicles are black with a white door and roof. The door carries the CHP's seven-pointed badge, and "HIGHWAY PATROL" is emblazoned across the deck lid.

and identify a black-and-white police car. These officers wanted to make sure citizens didn't mistake their police cars for fleet vehicles driven by the local gas or electric company.

In addition to a specific paint scheme, each police patrol car has graphics that identify it as a police car, which may simply be the words "POLICE," "HIGHWAY PATROL," or "SHERIFF" on the side or trunk. Most departments use the driver's door to display a departmental shield or city seal, while the 911 emergency phone number is often displayed on a fender. Marked police cars typically have a unit number painted in large letters on the roof, which allows a police helicopter to easily identify a particular car from the air.

Emergency Lights

Since the 1920s, red lights have designated an emergency vehicle. These vehicles carried one or more fixed forward-facing red lights. The first rotating red beacon was marketed in 1948 by Federal Signal Company. The once-static red light now revolved in a dome that was aptly nicknamed a "gumball machine." Also at this time, many of the forward-facing red lights were programmed to flash on and off. The rotating and flashing lights made the police and other emergency vehicles easier to identify.

Blue lights in combination with red lights became popular in the early 1970s. Studies had shown that red lights were easier to recognize in the daylight, and blue lights were easier to

Many departments have abandoned the traditional black-and-white patrol car for a brighter color scheme. This Ford Crown Vic is painted white with a laser-style tape stripe down each side. The unit number, city identification, and 911 emergency reminder are all displayed on the deck lid.

Lightbars come in a variety of shapes and sizes. The lights contained within are either halogen, strobe, or a combination of the two. The small white fixture on the forward edge of the roof is the Global Positioning System (GPS) antenna.

spot at night. These lights were usually mounted on top of the vehicle as a pair of rotating beacons, one red and one blue. Soon these rotating beacons, along with a siren, were housed in a single assembly known as a lightbar, a roof-mounted fixture containing several emergency lights. Since the early 1970s, lightbars have been manufactured in many different shapes with rotating- and flashing-light combinations.

Lightbars are standard equipment today on most police cars. There are a few departments, steeped in tradition, that have avidly preserved the red rotating beacon. There are also a few police cars on the road without any emergency lights on the roof, which, for obvious reasons, are called "slick tops." Because of liability issues, most departments are shying away from the slick-top look and installing lightbars in order to be more easily recognized as emergency vehicles.

Within each lightbar there are either halogen bulbs, strobe lights, or a combination of both. Halogen bulbs average 55 watts of power and can be mounted in a fixed position or in a rotator, which contains mirrors to direct and enhance the projected flashes of light. The number of lights and the rotational speed of each light determines the number of flashes per minute. Some lightbars produce over 1,000 flashes per minute or have two different speeds of rotation for the halogen lights to produce a kaleidoscopic effect that's hard to miss. To attain the specified color, the halogen lights are placed inside a red, blue, or clear plastic cover.

Strobe lights can be mixed with halogen lights within a lightbar or used exclusively. Like the halogen lights, the strobes are covered with a red, blue, or clear cover. A power supply is required to provide power to the strobes, and the power supply's output can be programmed to produce a selection of strobe effects that varies the intensity and timing of the strobe flashes. The varying intensity and timing of the emergency lights quickly draw the attention of citizens.

These various types of lights found on lightbars are used in many different kinds of situations. For example, fixed, forward-facing, clear halogen lights, called "takedown lights," are used to illuminate whatever may be in front of the patrol car. "Alley lights," clear halogen lights mounted on the ends of the lightbar, illuminate directly beside the patrol car, lighting up such dark areas as alleys, hence the name. Another option available is an amber "light stick" mounted on the rear of the lightbar. These light sticks can be programmed to provide a series of sequential lights to direct approaching traffic to the right or left of the police car, or they can display alternating end and center flashes.

This white Crown Vic is about as stealthy as the CHP gets. These units are used for commercial vehicle enforcement.

A police car running with its lights and siren activated is called a "Code Three" response. This slick-top CHP Mustang's emergency lights consist of one red light behind the mirror and the driver's-side spotlight (also red). When these lights are activated, the Mustang's headlights flash in an alternating, "wig-wag" pattern.

Departments shopping for a lightbar have a big selection from which to choose. Depending on the number and type of lights, a lightbar can cost as much as $2,100 and can draw as much as 45 amps of power. Along with drawing a lot of electrical power, lightbars also create considerable aerodynamic drag on the vehicle, limiting top speed. In recent years, the lightbar manufacturers have designed low-profile units to lessen drag yet maintain maximum light efficiency and visibility. Another problem with lightbars is the wind noise generated by the airflow over them. The resonance, noticeable inside the car, can be a slight rumble or a whistle, depending on the speed of the vehicle. The aerodynamic

design of each individual car also affects the sound produced. The same lightbar on a Crown Vic may have a different sound when mounted on a Caprice.

Recently, in addition to the lightbars, many departments have begun outfitting cars with an array of small strobe lights that use small strobe tube inserts (about 1.25 inches long) that can be mounted in any existing light fixture on a vehicle. All that's required is a 1-inch-diameter hole drilled into the reflector housing of a turn signal, cornering light, taillight, or composite headlight. Once the inserts are installed, they're virtually invisible from the outside. The strobe inserts are rated at 25 watts and are available in red, blue, amber, or clear. A control box is required to power and sequence the strobes. Because they are completely hidden, these small strobe units are often used in undercover cars. The compactness of the strobe light tube allows it to be packaged into other red and blue light units that mount on the instrument panel, behind the rear-view mirror, behind the grille, on the package tray, and on the back of the side-view mirrors.

Besides the lightbars, there are other lights on police cars that are also used for emergency purposes. Police headlights, for example, are often wired to flash in what is known as a "wig-wag" pattern, alternating illumination of the car's headlights at a rate of two flashes per second. This requires a controller that is wired into the vehicle's headlight circuit. This type of circuitry is also available to wig wag a car's taillights and backup lights at the same two-flashes-per-second rate.

Spotlights are also a key tool found on many police vehicles. These are often located on the driver's-side A-pillar and on the passenger

The lightbar on this Crown Vic has a siren speaker mounted in a chrome grille between the red and blue lights. The small white forward-facing lights in the lightbar are called "takedown lights," and the white light on the end is an "alley light."

LoJack

The LoJack detection equipment system installed in a police car has two main components—four antennas on the roof of the patrol car that receive a coded signal from the stolen car equipped with LoJack and the box on the patrol car's instrument panel that decodes the signal and detects the direction from which the signal is coming. The officer tracks the stolen car's location by following the direction indicated on the circular dial.

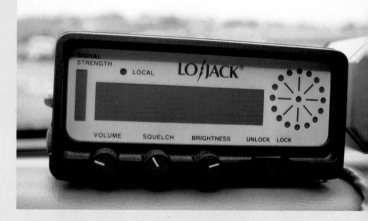

The FBI reports that a car is stolen every 23 seconds in the United States. Not all stolen cars are late-model luxury cars; the average stolen car is three to five years old. Today, the favorites of car thieves are Honda's Accord and Civic models; Oldsmobile's Cutlass, Supreme, and Ciera models; Toyota's Camry; and Ford's Mustang. Cars painted red are stolen most frequently, followed by black, then white. When cars are stolen, they are often parted-out, because the individual parts are often worth more than the entire car. Typically, when a car is stolen, it's only driven 15 to 20 miles to a location where it cools off for a few days prior to being transported or disassembled.

There are many ways to prevent a car from being stolen, the simplest and most effective being to lock the car. Other methods range from sophisticated antitheft alarm systems to devices that prevent the steering wheel from being turned.

For those who are *very* serious about recovering their missing vehicles, however, there are car-retrieval systems, such as LoJack, that will locate a stolen car. LoJack, which costs about $600 to install, works through a small radio transmitter (about the size of a chalkboard eraser) that's hidden in one of several possible locations on the vehicle. The LoJack transmitter is a completely self-contained unit that will operate even if the vehicle's battery is disconnected.

When a vehicle equipped with LoJack is reported stolen, the LoJack company remotely activates the vehicle's transmitter, which emits a coded signal once every 15 seconds over a range of approximately 5 miles. This signal can be read by LoJack tracker units that are installed in police cars (and helicopters) at no cost to police departments. The patrol car's equipment consists of a small box that contains a display screen and a circular light array. Four antennas on top of LoJack-equipped patrol cars receive the signal from the stolen car's LoJack transceiver and can determine the direction from which the signal is coming.

When the LoJack tracker unit in the patrol car detects a transmission, it beeps once per second and displays a coded series of numbers and letters. A circular light display indicates the direction from which the LoJack signal is transmitting. The officer in the car radios the department's dispatch center that a LoJack hit has been made, and the code is given to the dispatcher. The dispatcher contacts LoJack, and two things happen quickly: LoJack sends another signal to the stolen vehicle's transmitter, which changes the output of the signal from once every 15 seconds to once a second; and LoJack also informs the dispatcher of any information pertinent to the stolen vehicle transmitting the signal, including not only the make, model, color, and license number, but also the circumstances under which the car was stolen, such as a carjacking. In addition, LoJack lets the department know if any weapons were in the vehicle when it was stolen and, if so, what type, the location, and how many. Armed with that information, the officer follows the direction of the lights on the patrol car's LoJack display. The patrol car's directional finder is extremely sensitive to the LoJack transmitter signal and will take the officer directly to the stolen vehicle. Often, when a LoJack-equipped car is located, it's in the midst of a chop shop where other stolen cars are waiting to be dismantled.

side. Depending on the type of bulb, a spotlight can output between 110,000 and 270,000 candlepower of light. These A-pillar-mounted spotlights have a handle inside the car, which is used to direct the light. Spotlights are used as alley lights and takedown lights. They are extremely effective when searching a dark neighborhood for a street address. At night when making a traffic stop, officers will train their spotlights on the interior of the offender's car, once it has pulled over. This floods the interior with light, making it easier for the officer to see who is inside and if they have a weapon. Spotlights are also used at night when a witness identifies a suspect shortly after a crime has taken place. The spotlight is trained on the face of the suspect, making it impossible for him to see the witness. On some police cars, like the CHP Mustangs, the left-side searchlight is equipped with a red bulb and is used as an emergency light.

Switches for all these emergency lights are housed in a box to the right of the driver. The officer has the option of activating certain lights, depending on the situation, for example, a routine traffic stop. When an officer first observes and begins to pursue a suspect speeder, he or she uses no emergency lights, closing in on the speeder's car as covertly as possible. Once within striking range of the speeder, the officer may activate rear-facing lights to warn traffic behind that something is about to happen. Drivers are on notice to back off and be alert. When ready to pull over the suspect car, the officer will activate the forward-facing emergency lights. In police jargon this is called "lighting 'em up." This gets the attention of the offending driver. With all emergency lights activated, the surrounding traffic backs off and lets the police car and speeder ease to the right side of the road. If this stop were to occur at night, the officer would train the spotlights on

Today, small red, white, and blue strobe lights are being installed in the reflectors of a police car's standard lights. Because of their small size, these strobes can also be packaged into a fixture small enough to be mounted on the back of a patrol car's door mirror.

the interior of the stopped car. This allows the officer to observe any suspicious movements inside the car.

In short, lots of lights and an abundance of alternating patterns are key tools for law enforcement officers because they produce a high degree of visibility, necessary when chasing a speeder or rushing to the scene of a crime, and they help illuminate poorly-lit crime scenes.

Sirens

Just like emergency lights, sirens let people know that emergency vehicles are coming. Sirens on today's police cars produce a series of electronic yelps, wails, hyper yelps, and hi-lo tones. They operate through an amplifier to a forward-facing 100-watt speaker that is also used for the radio's public address system and,

in many cases, contains an air-horn function. Speakers are either mounted behind the grille, on a push bar, or built into the lightbar. Sirens built into the lightbar project a great deal of their sound into the passenger compartment of the vehicle, which makes it difficult for a dispatcher to hear a radio broadcast from the car involved in a pursuit.

In the same box that activates the emergency lights, there is also a switch for the siren. The siren can be controlled from that box, or, once switched on, can be operated by pressing the vehicle's horn button.

Sirens are especially effective on city streets where the speeds are low, and the surrounding buildings contain and echo the siren's furor. On an open freeway, however, the siren quickly loses its effectiveness.

The police car siren speaker doubles as a public address speaker. This one is mounted next to this patrol car's push bars. The forward-mounted siren speaker is favored by officers over the roof mount. When activated, the roof-mounted siren transmits a great deal of noise into the passenger compartment, making it difficult to talk on the radio.

Radios

Every police car has at least one radio. It provides the essential communications link between the officer in the field and a local dispatcher, other departmental officers, and a host of emergency services, including fire and ambulance crews.

Today's police radios have multichannel capability, scanners, and the ability to select a primary channel while scanning several secondary department channels. A primary frequency is reserved for everyday radio calls. The second frequency is considered a tactical frequency and is reserved for situations where a clear radio channel is important, such as during an extended vehicle pursuit or a hostage situation. The tactical channel gives those involved their own clear channel on which to broadcast. The primary channel continues to broadcast regular radio calls to all other units not involved. These other units are able to scan the tactical channel to follow the developing situation. Within larger departments, certain specialized departmental functions (SWAT, Investigation, Homicide, Administration, Detective, Bomb Squad, Training, Traffic Control, and Surveillance) have their own discrete frequencies.

Police radio frequencies are carried on four bands: VHF-low (30.000–50.000 MHz), VHF-high (138.000–174.000 MHz), UHF (470.000–512.000 MHz), and 800 MHz (806.000–940.000 MHz). A quick look at the car's radio antenna is an easy way to determine the frequency on which that particular department communicates: a VHF-low antenna is the longest, with a 35-inch whip and a 5-inch

Spotlights mounted on the A-pillars are versatile tools for the patrol-car officer. Controlled by the officer using a handle, these spotlights can be pointed in almost any direction. They are useful for lighting a crime scene, the inside of a traffic violator's car, or a dark alley.

This officer is using his patrol car's public address system to talk to an armed suspect in the doorway of a house. The car is positioned to offer the officer the greatest possible amount of protection from the suspect. *James J. Genat*

Opposite
Tucked between the bucket seats of this Crown Vic are the radios and a Mobile Data Terminal (MDT). There are two microphones—one for the radio and the other for the public address system. The large overhead light provides ample light for the officer to fill out reports at night, but, to protect police officers, neither it nor the other interior lights automatically illuminate when the doors are opened. *Dale Stockton*

coil at the bottom; the VHF-high will have an 18-inch whip; UHF will have either a 6-inch whip or a 32-inch whip with a 3-inch coil in the middle. Many departments are moving into radio systems that broadcast on the 800-MHz band, and these are the easiest to identify with their stubby 3-inch-whip antennas. Other antennas on the car may be for a cell phone, LoJack (see sidebar in this chapter), or data transmission on the MDT.

The latest buzzword in the police-radio business is "trunking." This refers to a system that shares a group of five or more channels among all stations and mobile units. Trunking allows for more efficient and secure radio transmissions. Today, all trunked systems operate in the 800-MHz band.

In addition to a primary radio, police cars often carry an additional radio scanner that monitors neighboring community frequencies for mutual-aid situations. Scanners are especially important for highway patrol and state police units that may travel through several communities during their standard patrol. By

The radio room where police dispatchers work is filled with computers and radio equipment. The dispatcher is the link between patrol cars in the field and citizens in need. *Dale Stockton*

Radio Dispatchers

The only communication a patrol-car officer has to the outside world is through the car's radio. On the radio, the officer can call in his or her position, ask for information on a subject, be dispatched to the location of a crime, or call for help. The faceless voice of the dispatcher is always there when the officer calls. Calm and composed, the dispatcher is always vigilant to the needs of the officers in the field.

All police agencies have at least one dispatcher and radio room with the phones, radio, and computer equipment used by dispatchers. Radio-communication rooms are secure locations with cipher locks on the door. Of all the dispatchers at work at any given time in a department, only the primary dispatcher communicates with the units in the field. Other dispatchers take phone calls and relieve the primary dispatcher during breaks.

When a call comes in to the station, a light on the dispatcher's console illuminates. If the call was placed using 911, there is an audible ring in the room that alerts all dispatchers that there is a 911 emergency call coming in. As the dispatcher is answering the call, he or she types the information on a form on the computer screen. Calls placed on the 911 system automatically fill in the address and phone number portions of the form. It's the dispatcher's job to get as much additional data as possible from the caller, quickly entering it into the computer. Once the dispatcher gets enough pertinent information in the computer, it will be displayed onto the computer screen of the primary radio dispatcher, who will make contact with a patrol car in the area and tell that officer as much as possible about the situation.

While the officer in the patrol car is on the way to the scene, the dispatcher taking the call may still be on the phone with the caller, getting more information and adding it to the computer file. The primary radio dispatcher instantly sees the supplemental information and updates the officer en route.

Calls coming into the dispatch center are prioritized according to their seriousness, in order to determine the dispatch actions to be taken and the expected response time. Priority One calls, which are dispatched within one minute, involve in-progress crimes or situations in which a person's life may be in danger.

Priority Two calls are dispatched within two minutes and are serious situations in which a person may be injured (nonlife-threatening) or a crime is in progress. Domestic violence, breaking and entering, burglar alarms, or fights are all examples of Priority Two calls. Hang-ups on the 911 line are also assigned Priority Two.

Priority Three calls are crimes in which a person's life is not in danger, including disturbances between neighbors, disturbances of the peace, or reports from someone who has just realized that their car has been stolen. Response time for Priority Three is 20 minutes or less.

Priority Four calls are for what are known as "cold crimes" that have happened in the recent past and for which a police report must be taken, including someone returning from a vacation to find that their home has been burglarized. Priority Four calls are cleared when all calls of greater urgency have been addressed.

monitoring a local frequency, a highway patrol unit is able to know of a nearby robbery and the description of the suspect's vehicle.

In addition to the in-car systems, virtually all uniformed police officers carry some type of mobile radio as part of their standard equipment. This radio broadcasts and receives radio calls just like the fixed radio in the patrol car, but they're typically low-power units that use a repeater in the car to gain power for broadcasts. Most police radios (personal and fixed mount) have an emergency button that, when pushed, will light up on the dispatcher's console. Help will be sent to the last known location as quickly as possible. This button is intended for use if the officer is injured or in a situation where he or she is unable to explain the details of the emergency. These and all police radio transmissions are taped and kept on file for future reference. For example, the dispatcher may replay the tape of a recent transmission in order to confirm what was heard. Another use for these tapes is as evidence in a legal proceeding.

Video

Anyone who's watched the evening news has seen the tapes from the police in-car video camera. These tapes have shown sobriety tests being administered, hair-raising pursuits, spectacular crashes, and suspects opening fire on officers. They show how a benign situation can turn into something deadly in an instant.

The camera for these video units is usually mounted next to the rearview mirror, for the best possible forward view. Most units have a fixed-focal-length lens, but some units have a zoom lens that automatically zooms forward to get a good view of the stopped vehicle's license plate and then zooms back to a normal view. The video system is wired to start taping when the overhead emergency lights are activated, or

The small white dot next to the grille-mounted siren speaker is a radar antenna. This patrol car also has a similar antenna that faces to the rear. These units can detect the speed of cars approaching and driving away from the patrol car. For an accurate measurement when pacing a vehicle, they track the ground speed of the patrol car while the car is under way.

an officer can activate the unit at any time. Officers assigned to cars with video cameras wear small remote microphones that record the sound track when the tape unit is running. The recording unit is located in the trunk in a locked box, and the tapes cannot be erased or taped over by the officer in the field.

One of the newest innovations in police video equipment is a remote camera worn by the officer that relays the video image and sound to the recorder in the car. The camera, which is about the size of a radio microphone, gets clipped to the front of the uniform shirt and gives a view of the situation from the officer's perspective. On a traffic stop, this window-level viewfinder records everything happening in the vehicle. It's ideal for a situation like a domestic dispute

where the officer may be in the middle of a large family disagreement. Recently, an officer who was wearing one of these cameras during a shooting was exonerated after officials reviewed the video. Many court cases have ended rather abruptly when a defendant saw himself on tape committing moving violations or falling-down drunk. The only downside to the video equipment is the long-term storage of the tapes, which must be kept on file because they're evidence.

Radar

Radar is an extremely effective method of accurately tracking the speed of vehicles and is usually installed in highway patrol cars or those assigned to a local department's traffic division. Today's radar units are compact and easily installed in any patrol car. The system consists of a signal processor-display unit that is mounted atop the instrument panel, a forward-facing antenna, a rear-facing antenna (optional), and a remote control. The type of radar used in patrol cars is Doppler in the X-band (10.525GHz), K-band (24.150GHz), or Ka-band (35.5GHz). Beam width ranges from 12 to 18 degrees, depending on the unit's operating band. These radar units are calibrated to track vehicle speeds from 10 to 210 miles per hour.

The signal processor and display for modern radar systems are contained in a box about the size of a paperback book that is mounted to the instrument panel. It has three digital display windows: target speed, lock speed, and patrol speed. The target-speed window displays the speed of the approaching or receding vehicle. The lock-speed window displays the speed of the locked-target vehicle. The patrol-speed display shows the patrol car's ground speed, which is used to accurately pace a speeder. A remote-control unit about the size of a TV remote control activates the lock-speed display and also has buttons to select the front or rear antenna.

For speed enforcement in a problem area, a patrol car parks parallel to the direction of traffic, either at the curb or on the shoulder. The officer watches approaching vehicles and selects the front or rear antenna, depending on the direction of traffic. Part of an officer's radar training and certification is estimating vehicle speed. Well-trained officers can usually estimate a vehicle's speed within 3 miles per hour. If an officer determines that an approaching car is speeding, he or she will activate the radar unit, and the approaching car's speed will be displayed in the target-speed window. If the vehicle's speed is in violation, the officer will depress the lock button, and that speed will be

Inside the radar-equipped patrol car is a small display that gives a digital readout of the violator's speed. In this case it was 89 miles per hour.

displayed in the target-lock window. The target-speed display will continue to display the vehicle's speed, increasing or decreasing. The officer is now free to pursue the violator with the speed retained on the lock display. Some radar units can also interface with in-car video systems, digitally displaying speeds on the tape.

One slick feature built into modern radar units allows the unit to go into a nontransmitting mode, thereby fooling radar detectors. Another feature of note is the radar unit's ability to discriminate between cars moving in a group, selecting the fastest vehicle in the group.

Many traffic units also carry a hand-held, or laser, gun. These guns are used to track vehicle speed using the same principles as the fixed radar. The hand-held units allow the police car to park 90 degrees to the flow of traffic, such as in a driveway. From this position, an officer can track speeders from either direction and can easily enter the road to pursue a violator.

The patrol car in the foreground has a video camera mounted directly below the mirror. These cameras are designed to start recording when the overhead emergency lights are activated. On top of the instrument panel are a radar antenna and control box. Many radar systems can interface with video systems displaying a violator's real-time speed. *James J. Genat*

Data Terminals

On the console of many modern patrol cars are data terminals. Some cars are equipped with an MDT, or Mobile Data Terminal, and others are equipped a CDT, or Computer Data Terminal. The MDT is simply a small communications terminal and keyboard that links the patrol car to the dispatch center and to other patrol cars. The CDT functions in the same way as the MDT, except the hardware consists of a standard laptop computer terminal that also carries the full functionality of any laptop.

These data terminals transmit and receive on their own frequency. Because the data sent is in digital form, anyone scanning the frequency hears only electronic chirping. For this reason, the data terminals are a secure way of communicating. Recently, one city was conducting a massive enforcement effort on a

group of local drag racers. The officers knew that the racers scanned the police radio frequency and then communicated among themselves with cell phones. The officers were able to communicate car to car via the data terminal, outfoxing the racers, and the effort was a success.

Another plus about data terminals is that they free up dispatchers from running information on drivers and license plates. Through MDTs, officers on patrol can access a broad array of information right in their own vehicles, without outside assistance. For example, using the patrol car's data terminal, an officer in upstate New York can request information on a car and, through a nationwide data-bank system, find out that the car was stolen in Nevada.

Important local information is also made available to officers through data terminals.

The interior of this police Camaro is equipped with the latest radar, a Computer Data Terminal (CDT), and radio equipment. Its forward-facing radar antenna is mounted behind the mirror, while the radar unit's display is mounted on top of the instrument panel. The small white device on the side of the console is the remote for the radar. Attached to the top of the console are the control boxes for the emergency lights, siren, and radio. The CDT is located to the right. Because of its location, the right-side air bag has been deactivated.

For instance, if an officer is dispatched to a domestic disturbance call, additional information regarding that call may appear on the data terminal. The officer may be informed that there were two disturbances at that location the previous day or that one of the parties has a restraining order against the other. This supplemental information gives the officer a history of events and enables the officer to better assess the situation upon arrival. If the data pertains to officer safety—one of the subjects has a gun, for instance—it will be broadcast over the radio to be sure the officer has the information. Other officers backing up the original unit can check their data terminals to read the information on the call. Also available on the data terminal is the status of all other calls that are still active.

Cages

Because patrol cars are used to transport prisoners, most are equipped with a barrier (commonly called a cage) between the front and rear seats to protect the officer from a prisoner. Cages are made of steel pipes and plates with heavy steel mesh in the upper portion. Many cages also have a Plexiglas shield behind the driver and passenger seat. The rear seats of patrol cars often have a special fiberglass seat that is molded to accommodate an adult seated with hands cuffed behind him or her; this type of seat also prevents prisoners from stashing contraband in the tucks and folds of a standard upholstered seat when being transported. Lieutenants' and sergeants' cars typically don't have cages installed, since they seldom transport prisoners.

The CDT is replacing the MDT, as it has the functionality of the MDT along with the capabilities of a laptop computer. This screen is for vehicle inquiry. While on the road, the officer can key-in the vehicle license-plate number in this vehicle inquiry screen, and the system will respond with the current status of that vehicle. A nationwide database makes this an effective law enforcement tool.

Guns

In the highly-publicized 1997 North Hollywood bank robbery shoot-out, there were 1,700 rounds fired. In this particular situation, two bank robbers held the Los Angeles Police Department (LAPD) at bay while they shot up the area. Both suspects were wearing full-body armor and had in their possession several fully automatic weapons. The LAPD was outgunned, and the robbers' high-velocity rounds were piercing the patrol car's sheet metal like a hot knife through butter. It was only through the exceptional bravery on the part of several LAPD officers that the bank robbers were finally neutralized.

Following that incident, law enforcement agencies nationwide took a long hard look at the possibility of this type of shoot-out happening in their jurisdictions. Many "what-if" scenarios were thrown out, and a survey was taken of the weapons available. Police agencies must walk a fine line in their choice and display of weapons. One officer, who wished to remain anonymous, told me that his department limits its officers to carrying no more than two extra magazines on their gun belts, because it looks "too militant" to carry more. This officer went on to explain how fast ammunition can be used up in a gunfight. Sometimes even four magazines aren't enough. He

More departments are equipping their officers with long rifles. This officer is checking out the 9-millimeter carbine carried in his patrol car.

also pointed out that criminals have no such restrictions on weapons or ammunition.

Today, virtually all uniformed police officers carry a semiautomatic handgun when they are on duty, including when they are on patrol in their cars. The first round is fired double-action (the trigger must pull back the hammer), and the remaining rounds are fired semiautomatically. Calibers range from 9 millimeter to .45 caliber. All California Highway Patrol officers carry the semiautomatic Smith & Wesson .40-caliber 4006 model, which carries 11 rounds in the magazine and 1 in the chamber; this is typical of the side arm most police officers carry. The CHP, like many other agencies, feels it's in the best interest of the

officer's safety to have a standard weapon. If an officer were pinned down and out of ammunition, the backup officer arriving at the scene could share his or her extra magazines. If the officers carried different calibers or makes of guns, sharing would either be difficult or impossible.

In addition to the handgun an officer carries on his or her person, most patrol vehicles are additionally equipped with shotguns or rifles. The majority of police patrol cars have a shotgun rack mounted (with an electro-mechanical lock) between the seats (against the cage). On cars without passenger-side air bags, it may be up against the instrument panel on the passenger side. Two of the most popular shotguns for police work are the Winchester and the Remington 12-gauge pump. Four rounds are typically carried in the tube, and most departments have a pouch on the stock with five additional rounds. A typical round for the shotgun is a magnum load with nine pellets of double-ought buck. Shotguns are primarily used when stopping a felony suspect. With loads of double-ought buck, the shotgun is a short-range weapon that loses effectiveness beyond 15 feet. Some departments use a round with a single-lead slug, which requires an officer's aim to be more accurate but increases the firing range.

Today, police officers are often forced into tactical situations where the range of the shotgun is too short and beyond which the average officer can accurately aim a handgun. Also, many officers patrol rural areas where they may be confronted by someone with a long rifle. For these instances, many police cars are equipped with a rifle, such as the Colt AR-15 carried by the California Highway Patrol and many other agencies, usually with three 20-round magazines. The range of the AR-15 is 1,000 meters, and it fires a .223-caliber round. Michigan State Police cars carry the Heckler and Koch MP-5, a 9-millimeter assault-type weapon used by SWAT teams and the U.S. Navy SEALs. Many other carbine-style rifles are also carried, depending on each department's perceived need. Rifles carried in police cars are semiautomatic, not fully automatic.

With all weapons, officers must qualify on the range every six months. Most departments also require that officers shoot every weapon in which they are qualified once every three months.

Shotguns loaded with double-ought buck are lethal short-range weapons. Some departments use lead slugs in their shotguns, which provide a longer range with incredible hitting power.

4

DRIVER TRAINING

Each party in a police pursuit has some distinct advantages and disadvantages. Criminals determine the direction of travel and what roads are taken, usually into an area in which they know the streets and feel safe, such as their own neighborhood. They generally have a complete disregard for the safety and well-being of innocent bystanders; they will do anything to escape being captured, including excessive speeding, running traffic lights, making illegal turns, and going the wrong direction on one-way streets.

While momentarily advantageous, this utter disregard for the laws and for the rights of others has gotten innocent people killed, and quite often, fleeing suspects have been killed by their own recklessness. The reason for such violent conclusions to pursuits is simple: criminals usually lack the proper vehicles and training for high-speed chases. Unlike police cars, the average passenger car isn't able to take the abuse of an extended high-speed pursuit—tires and cooling systems are usually the first to fail because these items are not designed for severe use on civilian cars. Also, criminals' cars

The vehicles used for the San Bernardino Emergency Vehicle Operations Center (EVOC) facility's skid pad have their wheels painted half black and half white. This allows the instructor, standing off to the side, to see which wheels are turning and which ones are locked.

Following a classroom session, these students, who have returned for some advanced classes, have been taken out to the track where the instructor (in the red shirt) explains the course and what is expected of them.

are probably not regularly serviced by trained mechanics, as police cars are. And criminals generally lack the driving skills of the average police officer, who is trained how to properly drive fast—fast enough to catch the bad guys but also with care and precision.

Still, not everyone can handle a high-performance car—not even all police officers. One of the biggest fears of some police academy cadets is that they won't be able to pass the driving test. They have the desire and intelligence to be a police officer but have never before driven a car at high speeds

for an extended period of time. To help prepare cadets, today, all police and sheriffs' academies teach driving skills.

In the late 1950s, as the horsepower of patrol cars increased so did the accident rates of police officers. Realizing the problem, many departments developed courses for high-speed driving and skid control. Most of these courses were designed by one of the department's senior officers. Often these early courses lasted only a few hours, and the training took place in a parking lot. Today, these basic Emergency Vehicle Operations Course (EVOC) programs

Patrol-car training even includes the proper way to drive over a curb without losing control of the car. *James J. Genat*

are highly sophisticated, with approximately 40 hours of classroom and hands-on track time. Each facility has a high-speed track, a skid pad, and a low-speed, precision-driving area. Refresher courses and specialized skills courses are also offered for veteran officers.

The typical EVOC program starts with a classroom orientation. Students are given an overview of the course content, a description of the exercises, a facility layout, and the facility rules. Next is a driving demonstration that shows the limited range of the siren in traffic. Instructors demonstrate defensive driving, with an emphasis on stopping distances at different speeds. Also taught are basic automotive mechanical skills such as tire changing, checking engine and transmission fluid levels, checking belts and hoses for wear, and recognizing potential mechanical problems. In the classroom, in-depth lectures cover performance-driving theory and techniques, vehicle acceleration, weight transfer during braking, maneuvering, and establishing a high-visual horizon. CHP Officer Dave Dreher elaborates on the importance of the latter, "The one thing that they taught us that sticks with all of us is what they call the 'high-visual horizon,'" he says. "Keep your eyes up—it's so simple to do. Most people, when they're driving down the freeway, just focus on the car in front of them. They're completely unaware that there may be an accident ahead. By getting your eyes up away from the taillights and looking through the windows of the car in front of you, you can see one-quarter to one-half mile ahead."

The nose-down attitude on this Crown Vic indicates that this student is using "threshold braking" prior to turning to his left. Threshold braking is where the driver applies the brakes to slow the car while still going straight and then drives through the turn with power applied.

Skid control is another important aspect of EVOC training. Regardless of the road surface, a car will go into a slide because of any number of factors, including speed, road surface, weight transfer, tires, and driver input. Instructors teach students how to safely recover from a skid by reacting correctly. Students learn that it's critical for the front wheels to continue rolling; if the wheels lock up—no matter what the surface—a skid will ensue. If the car begins to skid, students are advised to let off the brake or back off the throttle and turn in the direction of the slide. The driver must countersteer quickly and effectively to compensate for the skid, because if the rear swings out more than 25 degrees in either direction, no amount of countersteering will recover it. On a front-wheel-drive vehicle, power can be added to recover from a rear-wheel slide. San Bernardino EVOC instructor Scott Mahler's final words to his class on skid control are, "Don't make an enemy out of your patrol car." In other words, keep the car under control, and you'll stay out of trouble.

Skid control is practiced on the skid pad, which is an 80,000-square-foot smooth concrete slab flooded with water. The coefficient of friction on the skid pad is approximately 15 percent, whereas dry highway pavement has a coefficient of friction between 75 to 95 percent. On the skid pad, officers are taught not to give up control of the car but to use the laws of physics to their advantage. "At the CHP Academy," says CHP Officer Dave Dreher, "they taught us some basic physics on what certain steering inputs will do to the dynamics of the car. We were taught about the importance of steering input at the right time and how a suspension works. We were also taught how you can use it to your advantage when the weight is loading and unloading on the suspension. You really learn that on the skid pad.

Police work takes place in inclement weather and so does the training at the Michigan State Police Precision Driving Facility. Police officers need to have confidence in their skills and the car's capabilities in all types of weather. *James J. Genat*

You feel the weight of the car in the seat of your pants. When you're in a full-lock slide—but under control—you can feel when that suspension is telling you that you're just about maxed out and beyond your point of no return—you better start adding a little more steering input in the opposite direction."

Training on the skid pad not only teaches officers how to react when skidding, but also how to keep a level head. "You get kind of confident knowing you're going to skid and that it's okay to skid," says CHP Officer Dave Ellison. "You don't panic when you skid, because

that's part of what the car does, and you can still drive the car through the skid."

Another portion of every EVOC course is learning how to drive and handle a patrol car at high speeds, including "Code Three" (emergency lights and siren) driving procedures. The first laps are taken with an instructor at the wheel explaining high-speed vehicle dynamics, during which time students are taught about threshold braking and cutting the apex of a turn. Then the students get behind the wheel with the instructor in the passenger seat. When CHP Officer Dave Ellison

High-speed training is an important part of any police officer's training. This Michigan State Police Caprice is equipped with a roll bar and driver shoulder harness. The driver is wearing a helmet and a rather serious look on his face. *James J. Genat*

drove the high-speed portion of the track, his instructor felt he wasn't aggressive enough. "I wasn't really pushing hard enough," says Ellison. "The instructor put his foot on top of my foot and said, 'When I say push it, I mean push it.' So he floors it for me, and we took off. He pushed it and held it! We were going around these turns, and my two options were either go off the track or drive the car. So obviously I'm doing the latter, and I'm driving the car as best I can. When we stopped, he said, 'Good job. That's what I want.'"

Officer Ellison went on to explain that one of the requirements for graduation is driving the high-speed track in a certain amount of time while meeting certain other requirements. "When you get ready for the grading process at the Academy, they give you a couple of warm-up laps," says Ellison. "So I made my first two laps with an average speed of 105 to 110 miles per hour. You have a good variety of speeds on the track. Through the cones it may be 85 miles per hour, and on the straight it may be as high as 120. The second time through my instructor said, 'You're driving okay, but you're not pushing it hard enough—push it harder.' I'm thinking back to when he pushed on the accelerator, so I said, 'What the hell. I'm really going to push it.' I'm comin' into this one turn, and I pictured where I could cut the apex and still come out a little bit high and be fine, the same as I'd been doing. I was in this mental state where I was going to show him that I could push it through this turn. So I enter at about 95 miles per hour and probably the safe speed was about 80, or somewhere around there, because you never look at your speedometer. You're going for feel and where you were positioned the last time through. I had the same position entering the turn as last time, except this time I had about 15 more miles per hour of speed. So I just calculated where I should be on the turn. Consequently, I ended up going into a slide, and I started to countersteer to come back around out of the slide. But I couldn't. I was going too fast, and I couldn't get it back. I continued to slide, and all four tires were smoking. I went off the road into the dirt and came to a stop. The inside of the car was filled with smoke and dust. I could hardly breathe. I was gasping for air, and the instructor comes on the radio and says, 'I guess you pushed it on this one, didn't you!'" Officer Ellison passed the high-speed portion because he had driven so well on the previous two laps. The instructor wanted to see how much more he would push it. "There's that point where you push a car to its limits, and you need to know what happens beyond that point," says Ellison.

One of the newest techniques taught to EVOC students is shuffle steering, where the driver turns with short movements with both hands in a shuffling motion on the bottom half of the steering wheel, below the 9 and 3 o'clock positions on the steering wheel. The days of crossing arm-over-arm in a turn are long gone. With shuffle steering, one hand is always on the steering wheel, for safety. The other benefit of shuffle steering is that it keeps the driver's arms away from the air-bag deployment zone, to prevent them from being blown back into the driver's face or up against part of the car's interior structure if the bag deploys, either of which would result in additional injuries.

Once all these techniques have been mastered in training and the required tests are passed, new officers are placed in the field where they continue to receive instruction from a field training officer (FTO), who teaches the new officers the practical application of what they have learned.

Previous pages
Police cars are extremely durable. This 1990 Crown Vic can still thrill students on San Bernardino EVOC's high-speed track.

Opposite
In this drill, the student in the patrol car drives down a single lane that branches into three lanes with signal lights overhead. At a predetermined point, one of the signal lights will turn green and the others red. The student's objective is to transition the patrol car smoothly into the lane with the green light. In this case, all the lights turned red. Surprise!

Driving Simulator

After participating in numerous ride-alongs, I wanted to get a first-hand look at how officers were trained to handle a police car. To do this, I visited one of the premier training facilities in the nation, the San Bernardino Sheriffs' EVOC. There, the instructors were gracious enough to allow me to sit in on classes and to observe officers testing their skills on the track. I also had a chance to get some seat time in a virtual police car by driving a simulator.

Simulators have five video screens surrounding the driver plus inside and door mirrors in which objects appear and disappear. The controls are in the same location and have the same feel as a patrol car, and when you turn the key, you hear the sound of a car starting. It doesn't quite feel like a real car, but it reacts exactly like one. The tires screech when cornering hard, and there's even feedback built into the steering wheel. A loud "clunk-clunk" is heard when you run over a curb, and the engine sound changes as the car changes speed or the transmission shifts. The brake pedal even pulsates to simulate ABS.

The system is programmed with several exercises at different skill levels that cause students to make the same kinds of decisions that must be made while driving a patrol car in a pursuit. The simulator is very realistic, but, of course, it costs a whole lot less to crash a virtual police car than a real one.

Prior to doing an exercise to test my police-pursuit skills, I did one to get used to the simulator's car. It was a simple exercise that required a few starts and stops and eventually involved pulling a car over for a traffic stop. (Keep in mind that even in the simplest exercise, the system is programmed with buildings, pedestrians, red lights, buses, trucks, and other cars.) Then it was my turn to pursue—through city streets—a vehicle involved in a robbery. I started by observing the suspect's car in a parking lot. With some difficulty I activated the emergency lights and chased the perpetrator's car across a parking lot and out onto the street. I took a shortcut and drove over a curb and almost lost control when I hit the street. (Once the instructor saw the difficulty I had simply switching on the siren, he took pity on me and didn't require me to make radio calls.) The chase went through city streets, and the perpetrator ran stop signs and stoplights. My instinct was to bury the gas pedal and go after him, but at each intersection I had to slow down and check for cross traffic and pedestrians. At one point, I had to decide whether I should pass a car on the right or on the left. In the real world, police cars in pursuit are required to pass on the left. In my exercise, the opening on the right seemed wider, so I went for it. It was a bad move because I ended up clipping another car but was able to continue. My first pursuit exercise ended with me crashing into a building after taking a corner too fast. The instructor, Bob Rose, was nice enough to let me try the same exercise again, and I was more aware of what to expect and did a little better, but I was mentally drained at the end.

Police training facilities have a new tool to train officers—the driving simulator. With five video screens surrounding the student and several on-street scenarios programmed in, simulators challenge the pupil to make the right decisions quickly when pursuing a vehicle.

Completed exercises can be played back, which gives students a look—as viewed from above—at their windows of opportunity to make decisions at each critical juncture in the exercise. The view of the scene can zoom in or out from 184 to 1,000 feet above the action. The students are able to see their mistakes, and the instructors detail what should have been done in each situation.

The instructor told me that there's one scenario in the system that's impossible for even an accomplished race driver to catch the bad guy. There's also one that has the student chasing a juvenile offender through congested city streets, for which the proper solution is to break off the chase. Catching a juvenile who committed a misdemeanor isn't worth endangering citizens and property. A good lesson learned.

5

ON PATROL

The role of the police officer on patrol is to be on call and ready to come to the aid of citizens in distress and to serve the community by enforcing the laws. For many officers, the allure of working in law enforcement is that no two days in a patrol car are alike. Some days, when little is happening, time drags, and the officers have time to catch up on their paperwork. Other days, however, are filled with action-packed excitement, the kind of excitement that makes the evening news. One particular kind of patrol stop brings this kind of action more than any other—the felony stop. High speeds, radio calls, flashing lights, blaring sirens, firing guns—all the tools provided by the modern police car help officers apprehend suspects who think they are above the law.

A felony stop, often called a "hot stop" by officers, is one where the occupant of the vehicle being stopped is suspected of a felony, usually meaning the suspect has stolen a car or is driving a car used to commit a crime, such as an armed robbery, drive-by shooting, or murder. When an officer makes a felony stop, it's a serious event that commands a great deal of concentration and coordination on the part of all the officers involved, including the dispatch

Police cars are usually the first emergency vehicles to arrive at an accident scene. Once there, the officers will assess the injuries and call for medical help. Other roles the officers play include directing traffic and documenting the accident for reports.

Following a short pursuit, these two carjackers have driven themselves out of road. The two pursuing police cars have stopped, and the officers have drawn their weapons. All three officers stay behind the cars for protection in case the suspects decide to shoot their way out. A vehicle stop such as this involving a suspected felon is called a "hot stop."

center. In a felony stop, the officers involved are reasonably assured that the person or persons in the car have already committed one felony and may be wanted for more. In many cases, these people don't give up easily.

A typical felony stop might begin with an officer seeing a car that matches a vehicle on the morning's hot-sheet list of stolen cars. The officer positions the patrol car behind the suspect car and confirms it has been stolen by calling the dispatcher or, if the patrol car has a data terminal, keying in the license-plate number. If the car was stolen, the

computer responds with "inquiry matched stolen vehicle."

"That would get my attention immediately," says Escondido, California, Traffic Officer Doug Sams. The officer then makes a radio call to the dispatcher: "H [radio code for the dispatcher] 231 Tom, I have a 10-35 [reported stolen] vehicle in front of me, California license 3NRP874. We're stopped at red light, westbound Valley at Quince."

The dispatcher then makes the call: "All units, emergency traffic PD one for 231 Tom at westbound Valley at Quince." This call gives

Whenever there is a situation where several officers are on scene, only one communicates with the suspects. If several officers were shouting commands, the situation would become chaotic and even more dangerous.

As the felony stop progresses, the officers keep their weapons trained on the suspects. The officer in the foreground has a 12-gauge shotgun, and the other officers both have 9-millimeter handguns. The car's emergency lights remain on to alert citizens to stay away and to mark the position for any other arriving units.

unit 231 Tom the primary radio channel (PD one) and identifies 231 Tom's location for all other units. All units now switch to a secondary channel for their radio communication, but they are still able to hear what is transpiring on the primary channel. The dispatcher then makes radio calls to the two nearest patrol cars and sends them to the location of 231 Tom. For officer safety, felony stops are not initiated without cover units. In addition to the two units sent to the location by the dispatcher, all other units in the area, unless they are busy with other calls, will start moving in that direction.

As the light changes, 231 Tom makes the radio call, "Now proceeding westbound on Valley, vehicle occupied by two white males." As the dispatcher obtains information of interest regarding this vehicle or its occupants, it is passed on to all units in the field. Important radio transmissions from the dispatcher are preceded by three beeps. This is an alert tone for the officers: "Two thirty-one Tom and all vehicles responding: this is a carjack vehicle." The officers now know that these aren't a couple of kids joyriding but a pair of felons who forcibly took this car using a weapon and are probably still armed. The dispatcher tries to stay off the air as much as possible. If something is going to happen, it's going to happen on the street.

By now, the two suspects in the stolen vehicle have seen the patrol car behind them and are formulating a plan. As unit 231 Tom follows the car, he continues to make radio calls noting his location and direction of travel. The

In a felony stop, the occupants are ordered out one at a time. It's always important to get the driver out of the car first. This reduces the chances of him changing his mind about being arrested and deciding to drive off.

Recovering Stolen Cars

Part of an officer's job is to be on the lookout for anything out of the ordinary. Certain inconsistencies, for example, will arouse an officer's suspicions. It might be a missing gas cap on a vehicle, which causes an officer to question: did the owner forget to put it on the last time gas was purchased, or was a locking gas cap pried off so a thief could add gas to continue driving after stealing the car? Officers watch the vehicle and the driver for things that aren't quite right. Is the vehicle missing any parts? Is there a broken window or a punched-out door lock? And what is the demeanor of the driver?

Quite often, an offender with a guilty conscience will become extremely nervous with a patrol car in the rearview mirror and may start to drive erratically. If the inconsistencies raise enough suspicion in the officer's mind, he or she may run the plate. If the plate matches the vehicle and it hasn't been reported stolen, the officer will move on. If the vehicle has been reported stolen, involved in a felony, or has an expired registration, the officer will take action and pull the vehicle over.

Police officers are also astute enough to know the laws governing license plates and tags issued by neighboring states, as well as those for Mexico and Canada. Car thieves will often put out-of-state plates on a stolen car, figuring the local police will not be familiar with that state's plates or won't be able to check the plate. But thanks to a nationwide database, a license plate from the state of Georgia can be run in Wisconsin. While on a ride-along as part of the research for this book, I was with an officer when he pulled over a pickup truck with Mexico plates, but it wasn't just the plate that caught his attention—it was the Nevada AAA sticker on the bumper. The two didn't add up. It was a small inconsistency that most of us might overlook, but not a sharp police officer. Many stolen cars have been recovered by highly-observant officers.

While on patrol, police look for certain inconsistencies on vehicles that may indicate it has been stolen: a broken window, a punched-out door lock, or a license plate that has been altered are all red flags.

The driver of the car has been ordered to walk backward to the sound of the police officer's voice. He's then ordered to lie flat on the ground. One of the officers will advance to cuff the suspect and place him in the back of one of the cars. The officer on the right will cover that officer while the officer with the shotgun remains focused on the vehicle and the remaining suspect.

dispatcher repeats these calls, letting the other units hear the location and making sure it was copied correctly. The officer following the suspects will wait for a cover unit before initiating the stop; there's definitely safety in numbers, and the police want to keep the odds in their favor. Once the cover unit falls in behind, unit 231 Tom looks for a location to initiate the stop. If it's at night, the officer looks for a well-lit location. Day or night, the officer wants a spot that gives the officers the advantage and won't put any citizens in harm's way.

While the drama is being played out on the streets, the dispatcher notifies the canine unit on duty of the situation and current location of the units involved. Canine units are used to clear cars and chase or locate hiding suspects. The dispatcher also alerts the highway patrol and adjacent community police agencies, in addition to inquiring about the availability of any police air units. If the suspects decide to run, all bases need to be covered.

Upon finding a suitable location and knowing that cover cars are behind, 231 Tom initiates the stop by activating the overhead lights on the patrol car. In real life, the police like to have these matters closed out as quickly and safely as possible. High-speed chases make for great TV drama, but on the street they present a dangerous situation that all officers would rather avoid. In this situation, the suspects have decided to run. The dispatcher is advised, and the pursuit begins.

Now everything changes as the criminals take control of their future by evading the police. All police cars involved are Code Three: lights and siren. The first unit, 231 Tom, focuses on the pursuit, while the second unit handles the radio, calling out the location and direction of travel. The dispatcher repeats these calls to notify all units. Units that had been making their way in the direction of the unfolding events position themselves along the anticipated route. Most departments have regulations establishing the maximum number of police cars in a pursuit. They have come to realize that they don't need 10 cars following a suspect at high speed. These other cars are in position if they are needed. Often the suspects throw contraband or weapons from the car. Being caught with a weapon often brings an enhancement to the charges a felon will receive. The first officer directly behind the suspect's car makes the radio call stating the location and what was tossed out of the car. Other patrol cars in the area stop and look for the discarded items.

Following a short pursuit, the two felons turn into a small rail yard and slowed, boxed in between rail cars and the police cars behind them. As the suspects come to a halt, 231 Tom makes the radio call, "Hot stop, pulling into dirt lot, 1500 block of West Grand Avenue;

vehicle is coming to a stop in the rail yard." The dispatcher repeats, and now there's radio silence as everyone who's been monitoring the radio transmissions waits.

The patrol cars involved in the pursuit are positioned to avoid being caught in crossfire. There are no radio calls from the scene of stop; it's all up to the officers on the scene and the felons in the car. Other responding units make their radio transmissions to the dispatcher as brief as possible. As the units arrive on scene, the dispatcher logs them into the computer as being on this call. As these additional units arrive, they assume whatever role may be needed, including traffic and crowd control. In this particular situation, the fifth car on scene notifies the dispatcher that no further units are needed. This lets everyone know that there are enough cars, but that the situation is still ongoing.

The officer who initiated the stop, 231 Tom, is the officer in charge at the scene. He is the only one communicating with the suspects in the car. If more than one officer is shouting commands, it creates additional confusion in an already tense situation. The officer in charge and the other officers in the backup car draw their weapons, using the patrol car as a shield, in case the suspects decide to shoot their way out. The first command to the suspects is to shut off the engine and put their hands out of the windows. The officer's verbal commands are shouted loudly and clearly. The driver is ordered to exit the car slowly, with his hands up, and walk backward to the sound of the officer's voice. While the officer in charge is communicating with the driver, the other officers keep their weapons trained on the car. Once the suspect has

The second suspect has been ordered from the car and will walk backward to the police cars. The officer with the shotgun will continue to cover the car in case there is someone still hiding inside.

Before placing the suspect in the back of a patrol car, he's cuffed and thoroughly searched. While the search is going on, the officer on the left has lowered his weapon but has not holstered it.

reached the patrol cars, he is ordered to stop, drop to his knees, and lie face down with his hands out to his side. Once the officer in charge feels that the suspect on the ground is not an immediate threat and the other suspect in the car hasn't made any threatening moves, he will send one of the other officers out to search and cuff the subject. The officer in charge and any other officers on scene do

Traffic Stops

A key part of any patrol officer's job is spotting and pulling over traffic violators. While a routine task, it is not as easy as it seems. More officers are killed by other cars at a traffic stop or accident scene than by criminals wielding firearms. One officer called it the "moth effect": the more lights at a traffic stop, the more likely someone driving down the road is going to home-in on those lights and someone is going to get hit. Drunk drivers in particular "follow" any light ahead. But completely sober drivers have also hit patrol cars parked on the side of the road. Many officers shut down their emergency lights when making stops on the highway at night.

When stopping a car, the officer calls the dispatcher to give the location and the license plate of the car stopped. In case something happens to the officer, the department will have a location from which to begin a search and a car to search for. Officers approach all stopped cars carefully, even for the most minor of traffic offenses. As one officer put it, "Criminals drive cars. Quite often a simple traffic stop will lead to an arrest for a more serious crime." To protect themselves, officers carefully approach the car, watching each occupant for any movement that might be suspicious. Many officers only approach a stopped car from the right, where the officer can get a better view of the driver. With this approach, an

The officer standing to the right has stopped the car ahead for a traffic violation. The occupants of the car are prominent local drug traffickers and have been known to carry guns. As the officer on the right watches the occupants in the car, the other officer is calling for a drug-sniffing dog.

officer tries to keep the stopped vehicle's right rear roof pillar between him or herself and the driver when approaching. This provides the officer with a small degree of protection in case the driver has a gun. The right side of the vehicle also puts the police officer farther away from the flow of traffic.

Once the officer feels reasonably comfortable that no one in the car poses a threat, he or she approaches the driver. One of the first things the officer tries to ascertain is if the driver has been drinking or is under the influence of drugs. Often a quick sniff of the car's interior or the driver's breath is enough to indicate if what started as a simple traffic stop may have more serious consequences. The officer also carefully looks around the inside of the car for any sign of weapons, drugs, or alcohol.

In addition, the officer observes the driver's demeanor. If the person stopped for a routine traffic violation seems extremely nervous, maybe there's a reason (other than the frustration of getting a ticket). Often the officer asks, while looking at the driver's license, "Where do you live?" or "What kind of car is this?" Any law-abiding citizen would simply answer these questions. But someone with falsified identification may not remember the address on the license. And someone who may have just stolen a car may not know the exact model identification. Wrong or conflicting answers will raise the officer's suspicions and prompt additional probing questions. This type of good police work often results in felony arrests and the recovery of stolen property or illegal contraband.

It's not unusual, following a felony stop, to find a gun in the car. This officer has just discovered a .45-caliber handgun that was hidden between the seat and console.

Opposite
If available, a police dog will be dispatched to a felony stop. The canines are sent in to clear the car once everyone visible has been ordered out. If someone is foolish enough to run, the canine will quickly reel them in.

not relinquish the aim of their weapons on the suspect who remains in the car.

The suspect on the ground, now handcuffed, is helped to his feet and escorted to the rear seat of one of the patrol cars. The officer's odds have improved by securing one of the two suspects. The second suspect is ordered to perform the same series of movements until he, too, is secured in the back seat of a patrol car. Even though the suspects' car appears to be empty, the other officers keep their weapons trained on it—someone with a weapon may be hiding in the back seat or trunk.

If available, a police dog is sent to the car to search it. If a canine is not available, the officers will carefully approach the car to clear it, which includes opening the trunk. Once satisfied that the car is clear, the officer in charge makes the radio call: "Two thirty-one Tom, Code Four." Code Four indicates that the situation is under control. The dispatcher contacts the adjacent agencies to let them know the situation has ended. Radio calls will now return to the primary channel. At the scene, a thorough search of the suspects' car reveals a .45-caliber handgun stashed between the seat and center console. Also at the scene, a great sense of relief sweeps over the officers. The bad guys were arrested, no shots were fired, and no one was injured. It went down like an academy scenario. The two suspects will be transported to jail, booked, and detained in a cell until they are arraigned.

The officers are free, once again, to resume their patrol duties.

INDEX